# My Backpack was My Home

## One Woman's Wild Adventure
## Guided by Insight

### By Carolynne Melnyk

# Dedication

I dedicate this book to my family, who supported me in so many ways, even though they questioned what I was doing with my life.

# Table of Contents

# Introduction

For many years, my family and friends have repeatedly asked me to write a book sharing the stories of my adventures and experiences while living overseas. Since I returned to Canada in 2009, I made a few attempts at writing the stories, but it just didn't feel right.

Recently, I had a change of heart. Perhaps it was due to more time free time or the time was right. The little voice within that's been guiding me for 40 plus years began to whisper, "It's time to share your stories."

When I let this idea percolate through me, I wondered why these stories needed to come out. I haven't come up with an answer. I trust the timing of Divine Wisdom and therefore didn't question it too much.

In the unfolding of these stories, you'll come to know a very different person than the one who's writing the stories now. It's also possible these stories may shift, alter, or anchor something within you; or, maybe not.

I have lived my life a little differently than most people.

From early age I was guided by insight, or what I now call my inner guidance system. Sometimes it's a feeling: other times it's a voice or it's like following bread crumbs laid out before me. However these insights come, they never lead me astray. It's when I don't listen that problems arise.

As a young child I just knew things, like when someone was going to come over on the weekend. I would tell my mother and her response was always, "OK, I'll cook more food." Those were the days when not everyone in rural areas had a telephone.

At the age of 15, I heard a voice that said I was going to live and work overseas. That voice came with such authority that I didn't doubt it for a moment. From that moment on, my life was guided by an amazing series of synchronicities. A holiday planned for Spain got rerouted to Greece. An urge to add an English minor to my university education degree led to an organization that took me to Africa. When I was reading comments in a hostel guest book, it opened the door to me being able to travel around the world by teaching.

The more attention I paid to my inner guidance, the more doors were opened, the more direction was shown, and the more inner trust was strengthened. As I travelled the world, my inner guidance system often kept me safe, led me to incredible adventures, and introduced me to amazing people.

Some people may scoff at their dreams as childish fantasies. And others, who don't follow their dreams or signs along the way, often live with regret. I can honestly say I have few regrets.

I don't advocate that everyone should leave their country and follow a nomadic way of life as I did. I'm referring to listening to your inner voice and following it wherever it may lead. For it's by following that inner voice that we learn about who we are and we become comfortable with ourselves. When we listen to the voice inside us and trust it will lead us to where we need to be, we gain the freedom to be ourselves, to be free of fear, to be open to the beauty of the world around us, and to see the gem that each of us has inside of ourselves.

What follows are stories from my 25-plus years of wandering in which I explored the world's wonders and grew into myself as a person. Over the years, many people have told me how brave I am. I'm not courageous, special, or unique. I'm only a woman who's followed her vision, heeded her inner voice, and trusted her instincts that all would be well. Within these stories are also messages of the kindness, generosity, and beauty of people worldwide. People who are just like you and me, who are striving for a better, more peaceful world, and who are on the same journey to self that we are all on.

# Part One: The University of Life

I attended three universities, earning two degrees, and in my early years I had a fascination with higher education. However, it was when I ventured out into the world, trusting my inner guidance and coming into contact with people, cultures, and personal life experiences so very different from the one I left behind that I learned about living fully, which is an education that no university could ever teach me.

# Chapter One
## The Voice: Planting Seeds

Many years ago, I embarked upon a journey that would forever change my life and ideas. Little did I realize then, as I rode to the airport past the fields of large round hay bales, that my life would take many twists and turns. Eventually, these twists and turns would change my view of the world, change my view of its people, and change my view of myself and it would be the best education a person could have.

The year was 1983. I was finally acting on a message I heard in my teens "to live and work overseas." One sunny summer day when I was 15, I was sitting outside in the garden watching the clouds change shape. I had a thought, or what I call The Voice, which said that I would one day work and live overseas. At that moment, I felt absolute certainty run through my body.

Even decades later, I can still feel the moment when I knew I would do it. From that point on, I made my decisions with that goal in mind. When choosing a career, I intuitively knew that the field of education was my ticket to seeing the world, although at the time, I had no idea how or where.

I stumbled along through university and got married. I met my husband during my last year of high school, and we dated through my first university years. In many ways, I needed this stability. Shortly after we were married, my husband's work took us to Saskatoon, Saskatchewan, where we lived for two years. I did my best to be my mind's version of the model wife, only later realizing it was an act.

In 1978, the pull of the land and some persuasive pressure from my inlaws brought us back to Alberta. I agreed to this move on the condition that we give it a two-year trial. In hindsight, I knew that farm life wasn't for me. The upside was that the local school division hired me.

Two things helped me open my eyes to the fact that I felt trapped on the farm. My first prompt was a holiday in Greece with a couple of friends. The second one came when my husband presented me with papers to sign for land he and his father wanted to buy. I felt betrayed that I wasn't consulted about this decision and that my husband wasn't honouring our agreement of a two-year trial. This betrayal was the impetus that led me to take action on what was set in motion on the Island of Crete in Greece.

Greece was my first trip outside of Canada. It was like a dream come true for me, and I connected to the experience on more than just a physical level. I felt like I knew Greece. I felt at home. It was a feeling that I'd never been aware of before. My friend, Karen, who was travelling with me and who knew me well, commented that I became quieter and quieter during our one-month trip. Although I didn't realize what my husband, Karen, and other friend, Carol, noticed, I felt different with each passing day.

Near the end of our holiday, stirrings of living and working overseas resurfaced in me while we frolicked in the sea on the south end of Crete. I didn't want to go back to Canada. I saw and felt the world waiting for me. As I sat on the beach looking south, I thought, "Someday, I'm going to go there, to Africa." It wasn't surprising when I was on my way to my first overseas job in Nigeria four years later.

Synchronicities, or what I now call the Divine Plan, began to appear very early in my life, but it was much later that I would come to recognize them and allow this flow to guide me. A few more significant synchronicities would happen before I left for Nigeria.

In 1981, I left my husband to follow my vision. I decided to leave him after two years of inner turmoil. When we came home from Greece, nothing felt right anymore. At first, I was baffled by what I was going through. I tried to fit back in the mould of a wife. No matter how hard I tried, I couldn't put myself back in the mould. What I experienced in Greece let my spirit out, and it wouldn't be held back.

I accepted a job in a small rural school in Czar, Alberta, and kept my dream alive by scouring through educational journals and searching the overseas job sections for teaching positions anywhere in the world. Although I had a bachelor's degree in education, my major was social studies/history with a minor in physical education. Most of the positions I saw were for English language teachers. With this seed planted, a new trail appeared.

In the fall of 1982, I began to take English classes by correspondence. I quit my job and began to work as a substitute teacher closer to the city, where I enrolled in evening classes for teaching English. During these evening classes, I heard about CUSO (Canadian University Services Overseas), a Canadian volunteer organization. I was eager to learn more and headed to their university office the next day.

I discovered that CUSO could place me in a job with my teaching degree and English training. I was incredibly excited and, for the first time, really felt that my vision would come true. In January 1983, I re-enrolled in university to complete the requirement for a minor in English, and by August, I was on my way to Nigeria. I was heading to Africa, just as I knew I would that day on the beach on the island of Crete in 1979.

# Chapter Two
# Girl, You Aren't in Canada Anymore!

Arriving in Nigeria in August of 1983 filled me with exhilaration, excitement, wonder, and a touch of fear. It was the most significant culture shock I ever experienced. I was in a Third World country, and I was a volunteer living in a local village and receiving the monetary equivalent of a Nigerian teacher's salary. As a teaching volunteer in Nigeria, we were assigned to state schools in the northern regions of Nigeria. The state government provided the school placement, which was approved of by the incountry CUSO coordinator. The state government also provided housing and a monthly salary. Once we completed our contract with CUSO, the Canadian government gave us a gratuity payout.

For someone coming from a well-to-do Western country and a comfortable middle-class lifestyle, this experience tested my fortitude and conviction. It began the moment I arrived in Nigeria.

I arrived with the rest of the CUSO volunteers by air in Kano City in northern Nigeria, which is situated on the southern edge of the Sahara Desert. As we circled above Kano Airport, waiting for the ground crew to clear the runway of camels and goats, all I could see was a dusty golden desert and a few dwarfed trees. As I stared out the window, all I could think was, "I'm in Africa." I still couldn't believe that I'd left my home, family, and friends and was far, far away from all that was familiar.

The reality that I wasn't in Canada hit as soon as the airplane door opened, and I smelled that distinct scent of Africa. It's a smell that's still with me. No words can describe it or the special feeling that comes with it. Perhaps, in a previous lifetime, I was an African.

In addition to the smell, other things indicated I was far from home. A prominent military presence was situated on the runway and at the airport. Something unheard of in Canada created a sense of heightened caution with a hint of fear.

Kano Airport in the '80s assaulted all of your senses at once.

The process for entering the country was all very confusing: where to go, what to do, which line to be in, and what to hand to whom. People were jostling me from all sides, and there was a loud cacophony of voices, with airport officials seemingly shouting directions and names on passports, and CUSO representatives trying to keep track of us. Amongst of all this was the scent of sweat, the feel of dust and dirt, and the shock of unaccustomed, blazing heat.

After several hours, my fellow teachers and I made it through the confusion, heat, and sweat with our luggage in hand.

Then, we boarded a school bus with no air conditioning and few windows. Our destination was a boarding school. The school was our home while we acclimated and oriented into a new way of life.

As we barrelled down the road, someone shouted, "We're on the wrong side of the road!" Sure enough, I looked out the front window to see cars coming at us. The cars parted, and our bus passed through and wandered over to the right side of the road. We all sat down, stunned but safe. Welcome to driving in Nigeria!

I soon absorbed the sights coming at me through the side window. People were walking everywhere! Women in brightly coloured clothes walked regally along with bundles, bags, and pots perched on their heads. Men in long, colourful robes were striding on the side of the road, people were riding by on bicycles, and goats and camels were ambling along. In the background were tan adobe huts surrounded by tan adobe walls.

Tiny shops consisting of a few boards and corrugated iron roofs were displaying a small array of items, and women were selling little piles of vegetables neatly arranged on a bright cloth.

When we entered the city proper, there were more people, cars, goats, and houses of every description. I'm very visual and have always loved to be a passenger in a vehicle and watch things go by, but even for me it was sensory overload.

We eventually reached our destination, a government girls' boarding school that would be home during our orientation. I don't know what I expected, but what greeted me tested my resolve, and for the first time I wondered what I was doing there. I was tired, jetlagged, and overwhelmed, and now I was in a boarding school, which was dirty and run down by my Western standards.

After veteran CUSO volunteers welcomed us, explained the itinerary, and gave us a tour of the facilities, they took us to our rooms. Here, my heart sank. Suddenly, the image I'd created in my mind burst, and the reality of the situation finally hit. I felt a sense of being let down, by whom I'm not sure.

In front of me were two sets of metal bunk beds with very thin, grey, dingy foam mattresses in a room with grey walls that hadn't been painted for many years, and which were covered with the dirt of the many students who passed through. The volunteers handed us mosquito nets, a colourful cloth (which served as a sheet, skirt, dress, tablecloth, or whatever), a plastic bucket and a plastic cup. Then, they told us to make ourselves at home. The four of us in the room selected our beds, hung up our mosquito nets, made our beds, and shared comments about our new accommodations.

Once we had sorted ourselves out, we headed off to have a shower, carrying our bucket and plastic cup. Water in Nigeria was a precious resource. Although the hostel had running water, it was unreliable. Thus came our instructions on the proper way to have a bucket shower: fill the bucket with water and then, using the plastic cup, pour a cup or two of water strategically over your head to wet your hair and body. Shampoo your hair, soap your body, and then carefully use the remaining water to rinse off. It took some practice to use only one bucket of water. I was so happy I had very short hair.

During my two years in Nigeria, I learned how to conserve water by showering with only one bucket, being careful not to waste any water. I also learned that one bucket of water could be used for many tasks: washing dishes, then washing the floor, and finally, flushing the toilet.

This experience gave me valuable insights for accepting living in a Third World country and adjusting to different living conditions which has served me well over the years.

Thus began my adventure in Nigeria.

# Chapter Three
# The Honeymoon Stage

Mastering the art of getting clean with one bucket of water was just the beginning of what we had to learn before heading out to our respective posts.

No matter how good the orientation was in Canada, it couldn't prepare us for what was before us. It's only when one experiences something that one can fully comprehend that experience.

The first few weeks in Kano City were the honeymoon stage of culture shock. This stage goes something like this: a highly positive feeling, almost euphoric with everything new and exciting!

What could be more new and exciting than presenting oneself before the *Emir* of Kano? The *Emir* of Kano is one of Nigeria's most influential Muslim and traditional leader. There's been an *Emir* in Kano since 1805.

We were young, in awe, and impressionable! Everything was new and exciting. Even the oppressive heat and lack of shade didn't dampen our mood.

We waited for the *Emir* while dressed in our finest clothes. In the end, it was a short event where the new arrivals presented themselves to the *Emir*, listened to words of welcome and appreciation, posed for a group picture with him, and then left.

A month later, I had a similar experience when arriving at my post in the town of Shendam. As a newcomer to the town, it was my duty to present myself before the village chief. It was less ceremonious than meeting the *Emir*, but it was equally important because I was a foreigner living in his village, thus I was technically under his protection. More importantly, this experience made me a member of the community.

The next item on the learning curve was just as essential: the dos and don'ts of shopping. Since we'd make most of our purchases in the local market, learning market etiquette was crucial.

The first two rules of market etiquette were probably the most difficult for me. The first rule was to make eye contact and properly greet the vendor before looking at their wares. If you don't think this is important, let me tell you a little side story. After several months of living in the village, I went to the market one morning feeling out of sorts but needing upplies. After walking along the hot, dusty road for 20 minutes, I arrived t the market overheated, sweaty, and a little grumpy. I needed a few food tems. At the top of the list were tomatoes. I headed to the tomato section nd approached my favourite vendor; however, I broke the first rule of narket etiquette.

I bent directly down to the tomatoes before properly greeting the endor. When I looked up, she had her back to me, and that was the end f me purchasing tomatoes that day. She wouldn't sell me tomatoes, nor vould the other tomato vendors. That was the first and last time that I ever roke that rule.

This experience taught me the importance of making human-to-human onnections in any interaction with another person. It's a communication hat says, "I see you, and you see me." It's a small acknowledgment of our neness as humans. The person is much more important than any object ou may think you need.

That day in the market, I also broke the second rule of market etiquette: ou don't touch the wares until invited. When I reached down to the omatoes and began rearranging the two little piles, I was committing a big o-no. Only after you offered the proper greeting could you point to the roducts you would like and select which ones you want.

So much to learn and so many habits that required adjustment!

The third important part of shopping was paying. In Nigeria, you artered for everything, including a bribe, and there was a method to it. It lways started with a greeting in good spirits. It was like a game, and not ushed. If it was small items like vegetables, peanuts, cooking oil, eggs, or ooked food, it wasn't a prolonged exchange. It took time, patience, and uick wit when it was a big, more expensive item.

I often bought leather goods from one particular vendor who was ituated under a tree in the middle of a busy traffic circle in the centre of os, the capital of Plateau State. We bargained back and forth for over n hour while laughing and sipping tea. In the exchange, each of us told tories of how his wife and my husband (purely imaginary) would be so pset and what they would do if I paid too much or he received too little. Vith each addition to the story, the price slowly came down. Ultimately, it as entertaining, satisfying, and beneficial for both of us. This man taught ie a skill that would come in handy many times as I wandered the world.

The primary reason for shopping in our villages was for food. Shoppers ould purchase very few other things: Colgate Toothpaste, single rolls of toilet paper, canned sardines, canned margarine, instant coffee, tea bags, flip flops, cloth, soft drinks, and beer. People purchased everything else from the market in bulk, including salt, sugar, and cooking oil. Not only did CUSO volunteers need to learn the etiquette of shopping, but we also needed to learn how to cook with new, unfamiliar ingredients.

Part of our survival package was a recipe book containing recipes for dishes such as jollof rice, pepper soup, egusi soup, suya, dodo, okra soup, pounded yam, and moi moi. Our market etiquette lessons incorporated shopping for ingredients to make these recipes.

While in Kano City, the CUSO volunteers hosting the orientation also encouraged us to sample the local cuisine. These forays included instructions on the art of eating with our right hand while keeping the left hand under the table. Believe me, this way of eating took practice and was crucial to master. Keeping your left hand under the table was a way to train yourself never to eat with that hand. Most meals in Nigeria are eaten with the right hand. The left hand is considered unclean because it's the hand used to wash your genitals when you go to the bathroom. Being careful never to give or receive anything with your left hand was extremely important so as not to offend anyone. This was another very important bit of wisdom that was useful in other cultures.

To master these skills we went to local chophouses, which were restaurants often found under a tree, beside a road, or in a building. Some dishes like okra soup, which is often called draw soup due its slimy consistency, were an acquired taste that my palate never appreciated. There were also bush meat chophouses where I sampled snake, bush rat, and other food that remains unnamed (I didn't ask.)

I'll try anything once. Why not? You never know till you try!

From Kano, we then moved a little further south to Zaria City, which dates back to the 11th century and was an essential stage on the main caravan trail across the Sahara Desert. It also was the centre of education, with many well-established universities.

We were heading to this ancient city for intensive training in Hausa, the primary language spoken in central and northern Nigeria. In addition to acquiring a new language, there were many opportunities to explore this beautiful city. For over two years, I always enjoyed my visits to the city.

The honeymoon was about to come to an end. Once our language lessons were complete, the group dispersed, with each of us heading to our assigned state and post.

We were about to experience the culture shock stages of frustration, adjustment, and acceptance.

# Chapter Four
# Frustration and Adjustment

From Zaria City, those of us heading to Plateau State loaded our luggage onto a minivan and waved goodbye. As with every road trip in Nigeria, one must expect the unexpected. On this road trip, the unexpected was a military roadblock. Once more, we were in the presence of soldiers and guns. They stopped us and checked our documentation. Then, negotiations began between our group leader and the soldiers as to whether we had to unload our luggage for inspection. These check points were a way for the soldiers to augment their salary by demanding a bribe before letting you proceed. The tension was high, and fear was building as we stood around in the hot sun and waited to be allowed to proceed. Finally, with great relief, the soldiers allowed us to go. Everyone gave a collective sigh of relief as we drove down the road. In the 1980s, these military checkpoints were common when travelling in Nigeria.

As our group of teachers neared Jos, the capital of Plateau State, we could feel ourselves finally getting closer to our posting and our new homes. The honeymoon period was wearing thin, and we were ready to unpack, settle in, and go to work.

Hang on there, not so quick! Nothing in Nigeria moves quickly.

Didn't I say that the next stage of culture shock is frustration?

Upon arrival in Jos, we settled into the ECWA (Evangelical Church Winning All) Mission Guest House, thinking it would be just for a few days.

We were wrong.

We were about to get practice in releasing expectations and embracing patience as we experienced the bureaucratic system of Plateau State. Every day for a couple of weeks, we piled into a taxi and then navigated the labyrinth of Nigeria's bureaucracy.

For several days, we sat on the floor in the corridor of various government buildings. I gleaned three bits of wisdom from this experience. One: always have a good book to read. Two: have a supply of healthy snacks and plenty of water. Three: bring something to sit or lie on while you wait.

Finally, the paperwork was complete and we could move on. Each volunteer headed to their post, except for my posting partner and myself. It turned out that our assigned location didn't have housing. More waiting!

All I wanted to do was unpack and stay in one place.

Frustration set in.

Eventually, CUSO found schools for us, but we'd now go our separate ways.

Nervous? Yes! Scared? Yes! Wondering what the heck I was doing? Yes!

Now, I had to adjust to living in this new country.

My posting was in the town of Shendam. On a bright sunny day, a government official in a dusty, battered government jeep came to take me home. We headed south along a beautiful eucalyptus treelined road out of Jos. We drove on a major paved highway pitted with huge potholes or with complete sections of the road missing. We passed many small villages and towns with shops lining the roads, selling essential items like margarine, sugar, salt, batteries, flip flops, cloth, cooked food, beer, and soft drinks. As we travelled, vendors along the road played blaring Nigerian highlife music.

I was amazed to see people everywhere in the villages, travelling along the side of the roads, walking along footpaths in the distance, and working in the fields. Nigeria is a highly populated country, and these neverending masses of humanity never failed to fascinate me. One could stop in what appeared to be a quiet bit of the countryside, only to be surrounded by a crowd in less than a minute.

About an hour out of Jos, we turned off the main road and headed down a secondary road. The shortcut to Shendam! The road was narrow with patches of pavement and washboard ruts, which made for a rough ride. Despite the bumpy ride, the scenery was spectacular.

We had to cross a small gorge via a wooden bridge at one point. This bridge consisted of wooden planks, many of which were not nailed down but just laid over the metal frame of the bridge. Several of these planks were rotten or broken. As we approached the bridge, I couldn't believe we would cross it. I'm a country girl, but this was a little too much, even for me. The driver assured me it was safe, so I held my breath and ignored the knot in my stomach as we drove over. Amazingly, I came to love that little bridge and the shortcut home.

After crossing the bridge, we began our descent off the plateau and into the valley of Shendam. The vista before me was one of veldt, with thornbush trees scattered all over the place. Snaking through the veldt was a river. During the dry season, it was a sand path in which the locals dug holes to collect water that would percolate to the surface. It was prone to flash floods during the rainy season or would become a raging river. I loved how it changed with the seasons.

No matter how many times I made the trip on this road, the changing colours and textures of the landscape bathed in the hues of light at varying times of the day and with each passing season always took my breath away.

After a dusty and rough two-hour drive, we arrived in Shendam, the main administrative centre for the district of Shendam. It had a hospital, a police station, a prison, a large market, and a military garrison on the outskirts of town. Within the area were also a couple of schools, and my posting was at the Government Girls Secondary School Shendam (GGSS Shendam), a boarding and day school. The school was about a half kilometre from the town in a gated compound.

We entered the compound via a large iron gate and drove up the flame tree flanked driveway towards the administrative building. During the rainy season, these trees would burst into a multitude of brilliant red flowers, obscuring the leaves. On either side of the driveway were low, one-storey, concrete classrooms. Most of these classrooms had louvred windows with most of its panes missing. Paint was flaking, large pieces of concrete were missing, and metal roofs were rusting.

As I climbed out of the truck in front of the administration block, I was nervous and uncertain about what I'd be facing in my new home and school. A tiny woman with a Scottish accent greeted us as we entered the building. Much to my surprise, this slightly built woman with a wrinkled face, intense blue eyes, and wild hair was the school's headmistress. She introduced herself as Mrs. Scobie and proceeded to take charge.

The house allocated for me wasn't ready, so I moved in with Mrs. Scobie for a week. It was an eye-opening week. I discovered that Mrs. Scobie came to Nigeria with her husband and their young family when it was still a British colony in the 1950s and that she had lived there ever since. She was an exotic mix of expatriate and native Nigerian blending into the ways of the land. Mrs. Scobie was a no-nonsense woman who was equally fair and strict but who also had a great sense of humour. We quickly formed a routine and a bond. Part of our routine consisted of arriving home each day from classes for lunch, which always started with a bottle of Star Beer, followed by lunch and another beer, a nap, a conversation, then our dinner.

Then, we went to bed shortly after sunset.

I had one day to settle in before I was assigned classes and expected to get to work. After several months of orientation and waiting for a post, I was ready. However, I hadn't anticipated classes with an average of 30 to 40 girls crowded into a room with a shortage of desks, chairs, books, paper, and pencils. We had no teaching aids except for two pieces of chalk given to us each morning and a black section of the wall that served as a blackboard. There were no copying machines, no way to make worksheets, no overhead devices, no educational films, or anything I'd used in Canada to enhance learning. All I had was two daily pieces of chalk, a couple of books, and a group of students. As a young teacher with only four years of experience, this challenged my creativity and ability. My greatest asset was that these girls were very eager to learn. Thus began my two-year teaching assignment in Nigeria.

In the two years I spent with these girls, I learned to be creative, inventive, and resilient. I found different ways to encourage learning and meet the students' needs. In exchange, these lovely ladies taught me patience, compassion, and acceptance.

I was now home and had moved into the adjustment stage of culture shock. Sometimes the adjustment was smooth, and other times it wasn't easy. And, I still had one more stage of culture shock to go through: acceptance.

# Chapter Five
## Acceptance

My house was ready. I was so excited!

After months of living with the CUSO group and a week with Mrs. Scobie, I was ready for my own space. Finally, I could unpack and get settled. We loaded my things into Mrs. Scobie's car and drove to the house.

My house was a three-bedroom bungalow with an attached garage. From the outside it looked just fine, but entering the house soon dispelled that image. As Mrs. Scobie proudly showed me around the house, the excitement of getting settled fizzled out of me like air slowly squeezed out of a balloon.

The front door opened into the medium-sized living and dining room and contained a wooden sofa, two chairs with dirty cushions, a small coffee table, a small bookshelf, a rickety dining room table with equally worn chairs, and a small fridge. The walls were painted an army green from the floor to midway up the wall, with the upper part a lighter shade of puke green. Mingled with the green was the accumulated dirt from its previous occupants. The linoleum tiles on the floor were chipped and curled, with many missing, exposing the concrete below.

OK, I could deal with this. Besides, the lovely French doors opened to the backyard and a papaya tree. Later, I also discovered a mango tree. Fruit for the picking, yeah!

Next, we entered the tiny kitchen. The small piles of sawdust near the door frame indicated there were termites. It was a good thing the house was concrete, for if the door frame disappeared, it wouldn't bring the house down.

The kitchen had a small gas stove, a plank counter, and mounted wooden board shelves. It was small but functional. Everything needed cleaning, and I wondered where I'd start.

The bathroom was painted pink and had a bathtub, a sink, and a toilet with no seat. Oh, and by the way, there was no water. Mrs. Scobie told me there would be running water for an hour daily. Later, I discovered it came on in the morning while I was in school. So, each morning before class, I opened the tap and plugged the drain. The upside was that the water usually only flowed for as long as it took to fill the bathtub. However, t occasionally overflowed, and my floors got a thorough washing. I eventually got a barrel so I could store water. As a result, I almost always had a supply of water, even when the water supply occasionally stopped for days or weeks.

The house was dusty, and the spiders and ants had made themselves at home, but it was nothing a good cleaning wouldn't fix. I felt a little better when Mrs. Scobie informed me that she would send over a couple of students to help me clean the house. Everything was OK, and I slowly began to see its potential.

We ended our tour with the bedrooms. The hallway and bedrooms were painted a two-tone steel grey and dirty pink like the rest of the house. It was in the bedrooms that all my optimism left, replaced with dread.

There were three bedrooms. Two of the rooms had single beds and one had a double bed. The bedrooms needed a good cleaning like the rest of the house. What really turned my stomach were the mattresses. They were filthy! Inside I cried, "How can I sleep on any of these mattresses?" I couldn't imagine sleeping on any of them, but I knew I had no choice.

Feeling disheartened but not wanting to show it, I followed Mrs. Scobie back to the living room. There she announced she would be back in an hour to take me to the market for supplies. After she left, I toured the house again, taking in all the details.

I made my way back to the living room. I sat on the floor, looking around me, and cried great, sobbing tears. Inside I shouted, "What have I done? What am I doing here?"

All of a sudden, everything seemed so very overwhelming. I felt so alone and discouraged. The enormity of my decision rained down on me.

As I sat with tears streaming down my cheeks, my inner voice said, "You can sit here and cry, or you can make a decision. You have two choices. You can return home or stay and make the most of this experience. You WANTED this experience! What are you going to do?"

I wiped my tear-stained eyes and knew I wouldn't go home. I'd stay and make the most of it. With the decision made, I got up, washed my face, and made a shopping list that included bright, cheerful cloth for curtains and cushion covers at the top of the list. By the time Mrs. Scobie returned, I was ready to go to the market and get on with my life in Shendam.

This moment of despair took me to complete surrender, in which I accepted the situation and felt at peace.

As a result of that decision, I made many friends in school and in the community. I found solace sitting outside in the evenings and gazing at the starry sky. I learned to love watching the black wall of an African storm come rushing toward me as I ran around the house, futilely closing the windows to keep the dirt out. I became fascinated by the immense power of the electrical storms, even knowing it would mean no electricity for weeks. I enjoyed dancing with the students in the rain at the end of the hot, dry season. I found amusement sitting in front of my neighbour's house in the dirt, watching reruns of *Sesame Street* on a black and white TV with other families in the compound.

I even felt honoured when the students asked me to keep the outside lights on so they could scoop up the swarming termites attracted to the light. Then I watched them roast the termites in my kitchen using my pans, salt and cooking oil. Termites have a lot of protein, and my students had little access to protein sources. Besides, when roasted and salted, termites tasted pretty good.

There were many ordinary moments of being fully still and content, and many extraordinary moments of being fully alive and vibrant.

Then there was the flip side when life wasn't so pleasant, whether it was due to Africa's environment or human tragedy.

I disliked being dusty and dirty for months during the Harmattan season. Harmattan was when the northeasterly trade winds blew down from the Sahara Desert, filling the air with a fine red dust that got into everything.

It was annoying always having flies on my sweaty back as I walked in the hot sun. Teaching when there was no electricity to power the fans was challenging as sweat trickled down my back onto the floor. I missed coffee, bread, cheese, chocolate, special family events, funerals, friends, and running water. There were times of loneliness, questioning, and wondering.

It was painful when a car accident killed members of our CUSO family. I was lonely, not hearing from family and friends as it took months for mail to arrive, if it ever did. I missed getting news of what was happening worldwide as my shortwave radio didn't always get a signal. As an avid reader, it was hard not having a supply of new reading material.

From where I sit now, I can see it as the yin and yang of life, finding my balance in the ups and downs of daily living.

That moment of despair changed my life forever. I know I always have a choice in any situation. The option is to sink into despair, or rise above it and keep going. We all have this choice. It's up to us to use it or not.

# Chapter Six
# They Don't Teach This at University

It was 7 a.m. I wasn't a morning person! Yet, that morning, I was up and ready to go. It was my first teaching day, and I vacillated between excitement and trepidation.

As I walked toward the administrative building for my first official school day, my stomach churned with nerves. Mrs. Scobie was already there, ready to introduce me to the staff and the students.

I stood to the side with the other teachers, or at least those who came to school on time. Several teachers were on African time, arriving late with loud greetings and big "don't worry, be happy" smiles.

My eyes took in the boarding students as they slowly made their way from the dormitories and fell into clusters of tidy lines and rows with the few day students. Later, I learned that each row represented a house, with a mixed-level of students in each house. The house system was such that older girls would take care of and help the younger girls with their studies. It was a hierarchical system that had its strengths and weaknesses.

Each girl wore a pale blue, shapeless, short-sleeved, A-line dress and well worn flip-flops. Nothing was fancy or elegant about this uniform. It was functional.

As Mrs. Scobie addressed the assembly and introduced me, there was a cheer of welcome from the students. When everyone quietened down, Mrs. Scobie returned to daily business. As I listened, I realized how little I knew about the school system. The Nigerian school system was modelled after the British system, and I was about to get a crash course.

I smiled as I listened. That confident smile hid the turmoil going on within me. My cocky confidence disappeared as a wave of uncertainty, misgiving, and fear filled me. Once more, I faced the enormity of my decision.

The daily school routine consisted of assembly at 7:15 a.m., addressing announcements, duties, praise, and discipline. I found the routine uneventful; however, it kept us informed. One aspect of assembly that troubled me was corporal punishment in the form of caning for serious offences. These offences included disrespecting teachers or students, sneaking off-site, letting boys on-site, fighting with other students, or having a *juju* curse put on another student.

A *juju* curse is black magic or voodoo. Occasionally, a student allegedly fell very ill from these curses, which were taken seriously by the administration and staff. If a student felt she was the victim of a curse, Mrs. Scobie had to try and find out who placed it, then make them return to the witch doctor to reverse it. As you can imagine, with teenage girls there was a lot of drama involved. I sure was happy I wasn't the headmistress of this school.

Minor offences merited extra duties for the student. The degree of the transgression determined which tasks were assigned. Cleaning the outhouses was the worst assignment.

After assembly, we had a block of four classes separated by a tea break. By the time the classes ended, it was midday and hot. The teachers dismissed the girls from class, who then returned to the dorms for lunch and a siesta.

Around 3 or 4 o'clock, the girls who were boarding at the school were expected to do various chores. Some students worked in the field, where food was grown for the meals. Others cleaned the dormitories, classrooms and bathrooms; washed dishes or helped in the kitchen; or swept the school compound. Yes, you read correctly. They swept the leaves and other debris on the ground into piles, which were then picked up and placed in a compost heap.

After dinner was study time when the girls could share books with one another, help each other with assignments, and generally prepare for the next day's classes. House prefects supervised during this time. Depending on the prefect, study time was well organized and structured, or it was left to each individual to do what they wanted. Often, this was where problems arose.

OK, back to that first day of classes. Once morning assembly was over, I went to a Form 5 classroom, the equivalent to Grade 9 or 10 in Canada. I saw a sea of black smiling faces when I entered the class. I greeted them and wrote my name on the blackboard, and then proceeded to take attendance. I gazed down at the sheet in my hands and knew I was in trouble. I had no idea how to pronounce the names listed. All I could do was try. I did my best to read their names, eliciting peals of laughter. If you think it was easy, here are a couple to try: Adefolake, Chibuogu, Ifeoluwapo! Overall, this was a great ice breaker!

The students were very forgiving and patient as they helped me pronounce their names. I got my tongue around most of the names with time and practice.

My next challenge was to find a way to connect the name with the face. Learning to recognize 90 plus names and faces was a monumental task.

But once again, it was the students who came to my rescue. I was slowly beginning to recognize faces, even if I couldn't put a name to them, as long as they always sat in the same place. One particular day, I walked into a class and noticed the chair in the front row was empty. I pointed to the chair and asked the class where this student was. One student piped up and asked, "You mean the black girl?" The first thought racing through my mind was, "Yes." The next thought was, "I can't call someone black; it's disrespectful." I stood there, not knowing how to answer.

Finally, I got brave enough to ask, "Why do you call her black?" The students laughed and replied, "Because her skin is black." For me, all of them were black. Growing up in rural Alberta, Canada, I had little exposure to people of colour.

What followed was a lesson on the different shades of skin colour. That girl was black, this girl's skin was dark brown, the girl over there was light brown, and the girl by the window had yellow skin.

Wow! Of course, I could now see the different shades of brown. Once I figured that out, it was much easier to put a name to a face because I started to see the various unique features of each individual.

My primary teaching assignment was to prepare Forms 4 and 5 (Grades 9 and 10) for the WAGCSE (West African Government Certificate of Secondary Education) exams in English language and literature. West African students took these exams to graduate from secondary school. No problem! I could do that, but where was the curriculum? What was a WAGCSE exam? Where were the books? How was I supposed to teach with so few resources? These were some of the questions that I posed to Mrs. Scobie.

I must admit that teaching literature for a government exam was way beyond my expertise at that point in my career. I expected to be teaching primary English language to middle school students, not preparing students for government exams. The pressure was on!

In my first month, I poured over previous exam papers to put together a framework for teaching. I was grateful for the school's past exam papers and their couple of good literature books. The exam papers were like gold! I had to safeguard them while they were in my possession, and then returned them to the vault in the office.

Not only was I teaching outside of my comfort zone, but I also had to learn an entirely new way of teaching. No handouts or worksheets; everything was written on the blackboard and copied by the students. This process was tedious and time-consuming, but it worked.

I learned to use a lot of oral work. It's amazing how creative one can be when one has no choice. I wanted my students to succeed, and to do so I had to find innovative ways of presenting the material to them. I'm proud to say that in the two years I was at GGSS Shendam, the number of students who passed the exit exam was significantly higher than in previous years.

In addition to teaching, every second month I had dorm duties as a dorm mistress. This responsibility meant I monitored the house prefects, who were senior students and had the job of helping to watch and control younger students in a school. I had to ensure that they were doing their job and that no bullying occurred. Another task was to monitor how well students did their afternoon chores. In the evenings, I spent time helping students with their homework. Then, before I returned to my house, I checked to ensure all gates were locked. Most of these duties didn't bother me; however, there was one job that I found challenging.

Each day while on duty, I was to supervise the meal preparation. There was very little variety in the students' diet. Breakfast was sweet milky tea and watery porridge. Lunch, the day's main meal, consisted of draw/okra soup and pounded yam. In the late afternoon, it was usually tea and bread. All the meals were cooked outside in a large pot over an open fire.

The first time I went to supervise a meal, I was in for a shocking surprise. I casually headed to the dorm area, rounded the corner of the cookhouse, and came to a complete halt. What I saw made my heart race and fear bubble up inside of me.

Around the open fire were two women stirring the soup with large wooden paddles. A couple of metres away, standing in a semicircle around the cooking pot and ladies, were vultures. I stood frozen to the spot. I had ornithophobia! I was afraid of birds from a traumatic experience with a rooster as a child. The cooks beckoned me over, but I couldn't move. Eventually, one of the ladies came over, took my hand, and walked me to the cooking fire. They thought it was very amusing that I was so afraid. On that particular day, the cooks had to walk me back to the gate, for I couldn't get myself to walk near the vultures. Even though I eventually walked to and from the pot easily, I was always aware of where the vultures were standing.

Walking into the circle of vultures was difficult, and the second part of this task was equally tricky. I was required to taste the soup. During my two years in Nigeria, draw soup, which was mainly okra and other vegetables, made me gag. I couldn't get that slimy soup down my throat. The cooks took pity on me. They didn't insist that I taste the soup and never informed Mrs. Scobie. It was good enough that I came and supervised the preparation.

Over the years, I provided the students and staff with much entertainment. In some cases, I laughed with them; other times, it was OK for me to be the source of their mirth.

Besides my school duties, I had two other responsibilities as a CUSO volunteer. As part of the CUSO volunteer team and the Plateau State Ministry of Education, I took part in writing a new state curriculum. We produced new books for beginner English language learners at the end of my two years there.

My other responsibility was to hold a monthly TEFL (Teaching English as a Foreign Language) teaching methods workshop for the teachers in the district of Shendam. At that time, I had no TEFL training whatsoever. Once more, I faced a massive leap in my learning curve and ingenuity. For these workshops, I combined my university training with what I was learning as adapted to teaching in my current environment. Much of what I shared with the teachers was foreign because their education had trained them to present information and not engage the students. Here I was, a young inexperienced teacher, teaching older experienced teachers how to teach. How ironic!

My university degree didn't prepare me for these challenges. Although I was inexperienced, I did have far more training than most of my Nigerian colleagues, and I was happy to share what I knew. The teachers were grateful for new ideas, and I learned how to be patient and understanding.

The time I spent at GGSS Shendam gave me invaluable skills, confidence, and trust in myself. I often say that Nigeria was the fourth university I attended, for it gave me lasting life wisdom, along with adaptability, acceptance, and patience. I learned to say yes to life and then worried about how I'd deal with what was before me.

Each of us is capable of so much more than we think. When we stop thinking and fretting and get on with it, we find out what we can do.

# Chapter Seven
## Receiving Graciously

One morning as I left the classroom and headed home for morning tea, Mrs. Scobie called me to the office. Getting called in at tea time was rare, and I was curious.

I entered her office, sat down, and listened as she informed me that there was a rumour spreading that the government couldn't pay us that month.

Not paying teachers is still a common occurrence in many countries, where education cuts appear to happen before other government sectors.

All month we waited to hear via the African grapevine if the rumour was true. The village had few telephones, but the grapevine worked with astonishing speed. It worked for everything: parties, car accidents, deaths, school business, unrest, and coups.

The end of the month came, and we weren't paid.

Not getting paid for a month wasn't a problem for me as I had a small supply of naira, the local currency, and some US dollars that I could change to naira on the black market if I needed it. I also had guardian angels. These angels were British civil engineers who had a construction camp about a kilometre from our school. They ensured I always had food, helped repair my house, allowed me to have my mail sent to their office, gave me access to their medical clinic, and took me river rafting and to other parts of Nigeria. They became good friends of mine, some of whom I'm still in contact with today. As a result, I wasn't overly concerned. Besides, there was little to spend money on and what was a month?

One month led into the second with no pay. A few weeks into the second month, as I headed to class each morning, I discovered small food items outside my front door. Sometimes it would be an egg, an onion, a tomato, a piece of yam, or a bunch of green leaves. Other times it was some beans or rice twisted in a piece of paper or a small portion of one of the local dishes.

These bits of food puzzled me. In my naivety, I wasn't sure why people had left food for me.

One morning, I happened to meet the *Madaki*, the local chief's representative, outside the administration building, and I told him about the food gifts outside my door. Very casually, he told me they were from the townspeople. I asked why. He replied that I was a foreigner without family in the country to help me. The local teachers had a family to rely on and help them get through this period without pay, but I didn't have anyone. The town wanted to help. I helped them by teaching their children, and they helped me by giving me food.

After I left the *Madaki*, I felt guilty because I came from a prosperous country and had money to supplement my salary. How could I take food away from those who had far less than I had? For the first time in my life, I became acutely aware of my privileged status. Yes, I was a volunteer earning a meagre salary, but I chose to be there and could return home anytime I wanted. I questioned my worthiness in accepting these gifts.

As I wrestled with these thoughts, I finally knew I had to humbly accept the gifts. This poor village in this country generously gave what little they could to a stranger who had come to work among them. This act of generosity bonded me tightly with the people of the town. I was part of the fabric of this generous community, which resulted in the 20-minute trek to the market becoming an hour of stop and start as I greeted and chatted with women from the village.

Even more than the honour and gratitude I felt for the people of Shendam was what this experience showed me about the spirit of community. The experience of sharing whatever one had with another spoke deeply to me. To share with no expectation, to give with an open hand, and to know it would be reciprocated spoke to the fabric of my soul.

The gift of generosity didn't end there.

At the end of the third month, the Ministry of Education summoned us to go to Jos to collect our three-month salary. Usually, the money went into our bank account; but this time, we had to receive it in cash at the Ministry of Education offices. Every day, we went to the ministry office, sat on the hallway floor, and waited to hear our names. By now, I knew the drill. I brought a thick book, pen and paper, food and water, and something to sit on.

I left Shendam and arrived in Jos at the ECWA Mission Guest House to find it was full. In the 1980s in Nigeria, there were no telephones or the Internet to make a booking. A couple of my co-volunteers and I found ourselves in a situation of not having a place to spend the night. All the places we could afford were full. After a lengthy discussion of our options, we concluded that we had one more place to look for a bed for the night: the Jos Club, a hangout for Western contract workers living in

Jos. The expatriate community was sympathetic and often generous to us volunteers.

When we arrived at the Jos Club, it was almost empty, and there were no familiar faces. We ordered a few drinks and waited to see if any of our friends would show up.

No one showed up! Desperation was beginning to set in, and it was late. We had no place to sleep.

The owner of the club had been watching us. He noticed something wasn't right and came over to talk to us. In the course of our conversation, we shared our dilemma with him. He looked at the three of us and offered us a bed in his house. We didn't know him that well, but we were desperate. Once we accepted his offer, he arranged for his driver to take us to the house and get us settled.

We were extremely grateful to have a place to sleep that night. It was far more comfortable than the rooms at the guest house.

Over the years, I've received many gifts from many people. Some people were rich, others were not, but I always accepted the gifts with gracious gratitude.

On the flip side of the coin, this experience helped me to be able to give from my heart and with an open hand, not expecting or desiring anything in return. It's an act of love.

# Chapter Eight
## First Christmas Away From Home

Where did I get the money to travel? Even today, I ponder this question. All I know is it has always been there when I needed it.

As I look back on my time in Nigeria, I'm amazed that I was able to travel so much on so little money. My first trip outside of Nigeria was to Lomé, the capital of Togo.

Several of us volunteers decided to go to Togo for our first Christmas in Africa. We departed from Kano City. Travelling to Kano consisted of waiting in taxi parks until a taxi was full, which meant there were eight to ten adults, kids, and possibly animals. On various taxi journeys, I had goats nibble my hair, and live chickens or a young, diaperless child dropped in my lap. Plus, there was always the pungent smell of body odour. The first thing you wanted after one of these long distance drives was a shower and clean clothes.

I arrived at the taxi stand early in the morning and waited for the shared taxi to depart for Jos. In Jos, I transferred to another shared taxi and headed to Kano City. In all, it took about eight or more hairraising hours to go from Shendam to Kano.

Nigeria had a bus system as well as shared taxi routes between the large centres and smaller towns. Shared taxis were often faster as they stopped less and carried fewer passengers, which made them marginally more comfortable. With both the taxis and buses, the real hazards of the journey were speed, other vehicles, potholes, animals, and people. I held my breath as I witnessed cars playing chicken with other cars and then passing each other with only a hairbreadth distance between them. I came to the conclusion Nigerians had only two speeds: fast and stop. At high speeds, the drivers would often swerve around huge potholes that had the potential to destroy a tire or worse. The other hazards were animals and people all along the roadsides darting across the road in front of these speeding vehicles. The death toll for both people and animals was high. Early on, I learned that the best way to travel was to sit in the middle of the middle row of seats in the Peugeot 504 station wagon and go to sleep. I reasoned that if I was going to die in a car accident, I didn't want to see it coming.

Once in Kano City, I met my travel companions at the CUSO hostel, a house in the suburbs. The next morning, we excitedly headed to the airport bound for Togo. We boarded a Sabena flight to Lomé, and we were like kids in a candy shop. For several months, we'd lived simple lives with few luxuries. The first thing that assailed our senses was the smell of coffee.

Imagine months without coffee and then the smell of freshly brewed coffee rising up through your nostrils and making your mouth water. I breathed deeply, letting the aroma slowly glide into me. But it didn't stop there! There was French bread, real butter, jam, and cheese to tantalize dormant taste buds. I ate slowly, savouring each morsel. I can't imagine how we appeared to the other passengers, but I didn't care. Never, in all my years of airline travel, did food taste so good. Thus began my sensory and gastronomic adventure.

Lomé, like all other West African cities, was a colourful, noisy fusion of markets, people, and music. The women and men on the streets and in the markets were a kaleidoscope of colour. As one walked the streets or entered the markets, one felt the vibrancy of life all around. Nigeria was also colourful, but being on holiday added to my heightened awareness. The one thing that Lomé had that Nigeria didn't have were supermarkets with an array of French cheeses, butters, sausages, baguettes, coffees, wines, chocolates, pâtés, and other French delicacies. Togo, being a former French colony, still had a strong French influence woven into its West African culture. It was overwhelming for us volunteers who lived in small Nigerian communities with only the most basic offerings in our local markets.

I wandered slowly up and down the aisles of the supermarkets in culture shock. There was so much to choose from that I could only look. After a short time the feeling wore off, and I wanted everything but didn't have the means to buy all that I wanted. Next was the process of deciding what things I missed and balancing it with what I could reasonably afford. Each visit to the supermarket was a well-calculated process.

We spent our first night in Lomé at a hotel near the city centre, and it was a little expensive. The next day, we fanned out to find decent accommodation within our budget. One of the team members stumbled upon a motel located along the beach but away from the city centre. For us, it was like heaven. It had inexpensive, clean rooms, a large garden area with a swimming pool, a convenient barbecue, and it was close to the beach. Little did we know that we had taken over a short-time hotel used by the local ladies to service the sailors from the port two kilometres down the road. This little tidbit of information was only revealed to us upon our leparture.

Although the beach was lovely, it was too dangerous for swimming as he undercurrents were powerful. We settled for walking along the beach, vatching the men fish, and swimming in the pool.

The garden and pool area became the communal meeting point each lay. It was there that I met volunteers working in other West African ocations and representing a wide range of volunteer organizations from around the world. I soon realized that within this motel, we were a United Nations of volunteers.

As Christmas neared, we began to make plans for the holiday. As a group, we decided to have a barbecue in the garden for our Christmas meal. We arranged with the hotel to purchase charcoal and to use the hotel lishes and cutlery. Each person bought their food and drink. The whole lay had a festive ambiance as we got ready for our evening celebration.

This day was one of my most memorable Christmases. After dinner, we congregated around the pool with representatives from Germany, France, United States, England, Ireland, Scotland, Denmark, Sweden, and Canada. A group of adventurous young people joined together in celebration. It was beautiful!

As the sun dropped in the west, the moon and stars emerged and we began to sing Christmas carols. One by one, each volunteer took turns singing carols from their country. We sat by the pool for many hours, singing and sharing Christmas customs from our respective cultures. It vas a memorable night of unity, harmony, and peace under the West African skies.

We topped it off by heading to the central cathedral for midnight mass. Although I wasn't Catholic, I'd attended mass in Canada, but it was nothing like this. The church had brilliant flowers, colourful cloth, and a beautiful, large nativity scene. Everyone dressed in their best clothes, adding to the occasion. But, it was the singing, clapping, drumming, and dancing during he mass that was most powerful. I couldn't sit still, and before I knew it, I was up clapping and dancing like everyone else. It was heartfelt rejoicing in he birth of Jesus. It was uplifting, sincere and reverent.

This experience has stayed with me all these years. When one experiences something so powerful, it's beyond words and only the feeling remains.

A year later, I witnessed this scene all over again but this time in Shendam. It was just as colourful, joyful, invigorating, and meaningful as it vas in Lomé.

# Chapter Nine
# Am I Going To Die?

Death is one topic that we tend to shy away from, and no one likes to look their mortality in the eye. But, life has a way of showing us what we don't want to see.

I'd just arrived home from Katsina in northern Nigeria, where I was visiting my friend Florence. It was a great little holiday in a town just south of the border between Nigeria and Niger. The city of Katsina was a tiny oasis surrounded by shifting Sahara Desert sands. Although the vegetation was sparse, there was a beauty in the stark openness of the desert.

As I unpacked, I felt refreshed and ready for another session of school. It felt good to be home and surrounded by trees and greenery.

The school week began as it usually did after each holiday, as boarding students trickled in. It would be at least a week before all the students were back. During this window of time, I gave each student more individual help.

When the weekend arrived, I spent Saturday hanging out at the pool with my British civil engineer buddies. Mrs. Scobie introduced me to them the first week I was in the area. During my time in Nigeria, these men were my knights in shining armour. They watched over me, helped in a variety of ways, and saved my life. One of them was my sugar daddy for a few years. It was a romance destined to be short, as my free spirit was alive and well, not exactly suited to join the life of a 60 year old.

On Sunday morning, I woke up feeling a little sluggish, and I put it down to spending too much time in the sun by the pool, or perhaps due to drinking too many gin and tonics. I did a few things around the house and got my lessons ready for the week in anticipation of full attendance.

The next morning, I still felt off. I had a slight headache and was stiff and sore. I didn't overthink it and thought it would pass. I went to class and did all the things that needed to get done. But as the week progressed, I felt drained and had a noticeable fever.

At midweek, I was curled on the sofa covered in a sheet when one of the students dropped by to bring me some of her school work. She took one look at me and took off at a run to fetch Mrs. Scobie.

Within minutes Mrs. Scobie drove up to my house, gathered me up, and took me to the civil engineer camp. Although Shendam had a hospital, it wasn't one you wanted to enter. The alternative, for us privileged ones, was the clinic at the camp, which had a triage nurse.

The verdict: I had malaria.

Before I left Canada, CUSO had drummed it into me that Sunday was chloroquine day. Every Sunday, for months, I took the chloroquine pills. They were nasty! Once I swallowed them, I felt nauseous and had an upset stomach, but I took them. Even though I followed all the precautions, took the medication, and slept under a mosquito net, one mosquito found me. All it took was one female mosquito!

I was immediately put into bed and hooked up to an IV. As the fever soared, my reality became distorted. I entered a state of delirium. I recall having thoughts flow in and out, like, "I don't want to die. I want to go home. I want to see my family again. I don't want to die."

I drifted from being aware of where I was and who I was with to the world of my inner fears, followed by severe chills and restless sleep.

For three days, I had cold showers three or four times a day to try to bring the fever down. I had someone with me 24 hours a day, and the nurse slept on a cot in the clinic. It was the best medical care available in that remote part of the world.

Gradually the fever subsided, the inner fears ended, and I began to recover. I remained in the clinic for a week, then was given a room at the camp to stay in until I was strong enough to return to my house. I returned to the school compound after a week of rest, and even then I tired quickly. It took a few weeks before my full energy came back.

I'm still grateful to Gleeson Civil Engineering for being there in my time of need. That first bout of malaria was a frightening experience and one I was happy I didn't have to deal with alone.

You read that right, I did get malaria a second time, and again it was after spending time in northern Nigeria. One would think that being on the fringe of a desert would mean there wouldn't be mosquitoes. Not so!

My second adventure with malaria wasn't as severe. This time as soon as I felt the telltale ache in my lower back, I took myself to the clinic for a malaria test. This test was quick and easy: a jab to a fingertip, a drop of blood, and an almost instant result. Once the clinic staff confirmed that I had malaria, they gave me anti-malaria drugs and sent me home.

Home was the CUSO house/hostel in Kano City. My caregivers were the volunteers staying at the hostel. They gave me a steady supply of fluids, brought me food, and ensured I took the medicine. They generally kept an eye out for any changes. Because I knew the signs and was proactive, the fever wasn't so bad and I recovered quickly. A week later, I was in a taxi heading back to Shendam.

Many of you may be reading this and thinking, "Oh my God! You could've died." Yes, I could've died, but I didn't. I'm still here 30 plus years later.

There's no such thing as "could have". Everything in life either happens or it doesn't. If it does, one deals with it. If it doesn't, why even give it any thought?

How many hours have you spent mulling over all the possibilities of what could've happened? Have you ever considered this worrying was keeping you stuck in the past rather than being grateful in the present?

From my many adventures, I've discovered that everyone has the strength and resiliency to face whatever life presents and to keep on going. You don't have to go to the farthest reaches of the world to see this; it's all around you. Every day someone faces unexpected lifechanging challenges, and the only way forward is to keep going. Staying in the past and ruminating on what could've been will sap your energy and blind you to the wonders that surround you now.

The next time you find yourself slipping into "it could've," pause and remind yourself that there's no such thing as "could've".

# Chapter Eleven
# My Tiny World Explodes

Greece, Nigeria, Togo, and Kenya. The free spirit cast her gaze on the world; where to go next?

I finally understood why my psychic maternal grandmother always called me her "little gypsy".

I was born with a free spirit. My older sister told me that when I was a young child, I stood on the seat in city buses with my nose pressed against the window, enthralled by the passing vista. When it was time to get off the bus, I'd hold onto the seat and create an enormous fuss because I didn't want to get off. I wanted to keep going and explore more.

As a teenager, I grew up in the late '60s and early '70s. When I heard or read about hippies going from place to place in a psychedelic van, something stirred within me. Even then, I had a longing for freedom, adventure, and exploration. Yet at that time, something held me back.

Then in my late 20s, I revisited all those inner longings as I sat on the other side of the world in Nigeria and contemplated what I'd do when my contract was up. Would I stay for another year or two? Or, would I head in another direction? Interestingly, returning to Canada was not an option.

It was while I was on a trip to Kenya in 1984 when the whole world opened before me. In Kenya, I discovered the life of a traveller. This was someone who meandered from place to place or country to country without a fixed itinerary or limited timeframe. I was enthralled! Here was my freedom, only much more extensive than my teenage version.

I came from a background where a road trip of a few hours to the mountains was thought of as a considerable journey. There I was, sitting under the famous thorn tree in the courtyard of the Stanley Hotel in Nairobi, Kenya, surrounded by travellers. The Thorn Tree Cafe acted as a notice board for news in Nairobi but also was used by travellers who left messages for each other. This hotel was the grand meeting place for travellers for many years.

All my limitations shattered as the world opened up for me. Once that genie, or should I say free spirit, was out of the bottle, there was no going back.

For a whole month, I was surrounded by these global vagabonds. As we sat around the campfire on safari, drank beer around the Stanley Hotel thorn tree in Nairobi, or laid on the beaches of Lamu, I listened as they shared their adventures from Egypt, Israel, India, and the Far East. Some of these people had been on the road for six months, a year, or longer. I was like a sponge taking in every detail. I felt my soul yearning to travel with no specific destination, only with a sense of adventure and curiosity.

These weren't seeds being planted; these were seedlings ready to take on the world. As if that wasn't enough, the universe had one more tidbit to ensure I was paying attention.

During our last few days in Kenya, we stayed at a hostel in Nairobi. One morning after I finished my hostel duties cleaning the women's washroom, I made a cup of tea and went into the lounge to wait for my friends. I idly picked up the guestbook and began to read. I read stories of travellers who passed through Kenya on their way to the next destination. But, it was the stories I read about how easy it was to get work in language schools in India and Thailand that grabbed my attention. The only qualification required was to be a native English speaker.

I paused and looked up from the guestbook as my mind raced. Not only was I a native English speaker, I was also a qualified English teacher. The door to the world flew open. I could explore the world and find work to support myself. The vision of living and working overseas was possible, and the door was wide open before me.

This mysterious chain of events that linked together one part of my life with another continues to be everpresent. Sometimes I felt faint little nudges or heard a voice, and other times they were in my face, not-to-be-missed messages. The amazing thing about them was that with my limited view of the world, I had no way to manifest any of these connections or where they would lead me; they just appeared.

From vast personal experience and from where I stand now, I see it all as part of the Divine Grand Plan. The Divine Plan that keeps me moving forward, stepping outside of my comfort zone, and experiencing the fullness of life.

I returned to Nigeria, where these seedlings laid dormant for six months. When I discovered my contract in Nigeria wouldn't be renewed, these plants came to life and I knew my next step.

But until then, I still had more adventures to experience in Nigeria.

Can you see the links in your life? Were they little nudges, quiet voices, or major pushes? Did you listen and follow them? Why or why not?

# Chapter Twelve
# Engaged Twice! Who, Me?

A wonderful thing about working in Nigeria was the fact that the school was closed for both Muslim and Christian holidays as well as on national days. This gave me plenty of opportunities to travel.

After the trip to Kenya, I taught for a few months, and then flew off to the United Kingdom where I was to meet my sister and brother-in-law in Manchester for a family holiday. I was super excited for three reasons: I would get to see my sister, I was going to England, and I could buy new clothes. Hand washing and drying clothes under the hot African sun has a way of destroying them.

I arrived in Manchester full of excitement and anticipation. As I entered the airport, I scanned the sea of faces looking for my sister and my brother-in-law with little success. I stood off to the side and waited for them to arrive. Instead of seeing their familiar faces, I heard my name being called over the PA system, informing me to go to the information desk. With a sense of foreboding, I made my way to the desk.

I was right! The news wasn't good. My brother-in-law's mother was very ill and they cancelled their trip.

All of a sudden, I was alone. I had no family with whom to travel and virtually no money. We'd planned for my sister to bring money from my account because there was no way to get hard currency in Nigeria. Thank goodness I had a credit card; however, in those days there were no ATMs at the airport and the only way to get cash from a credit card was to go to a bank.

With help from the information desk staff, I found a bed and breakfast that took credit cards and made sure I could get to it using public transport with the little money I had. Feeling a little apprehensive, I made my way from the airport to the bed and breakfast. By this time, I was exhausted from the roller coaster of emotions that I'd been on for the past 24 hours and tumbled into bed.

The next morning, with guidance from the bed and breakfast owner, I went to a bank, withdrew money, and started my two-week adventure in England.

I spent a few days touring Manchester and then a few days in Liverpool with friends who lived there. In Liverpool, my friends acted as tour guides as I checked off all the famous Beatles sites on my list. Next, I headed to London.

In London, I stayed in a bed and breakfast in the Bayswater area. Each day after breakfast, I'd go out and explore the city. I became adept at using the London

Underground and the double-decker buses as I visited and then crossed off all the historical sites I'd studied as a history major.

Next, came side trips to Oxford, Cambridge, and Stratford-upon-Avon. The universities enthralled me! As I followed the tour guide, I imagined what it would be like to be a student in one of these historical centres of learning.

In the evening, I returned to the bed and breakfast and stopped in the lounge to have a drink before I went out for dinner. It wasn't long before I became acquainted with a few of the local patrons: two men, a husband and wife, a Lebanese businessman, and the bartender. Every day, this group was eager to hear the tales of my day's adventures.

On the third evening, the group invited me to go out with them after the lounge closed. We headed off to a local pub where I could have dinner as well as continue to drink. This became the pattern for the rest of the week in London. As the week passed, this group took me to different pubs as well as a few member-only clubs in the area where we'd eat, drink, play darts, and dance. They introduced me to a part of London life that most tourists never see. I must admit that I did have a grand time.

This good time also included spending a few nights with Hamid, my new Lebanese friend. The last night I stayed with him, he gave me a gold necklace and we made tentative plans to meet on the island of Cyprus at Christmas. We parted ways and I returned to Nigeria to start a new semester.

Before long, I was back in my daily routine with London far behind me. When I received a letter from Hamid a month later with plans for Christmas in Cyprus, I was a little taken aback because I'd understood it to be a possible plan, not a fait accompli. Besides, a friendship that had started in Nigeria before the trip to England was now turning into something much stronger than a friendship. I quickly penned a letter of apology to Hamid and put the whole affair in the back of my mind.

Two-and-a-half years later, I returned to London for a job fair and stayed at the same bed and breakfast in Bayswater. After I checked in and took my backpack to my room, I went into the bar to see if the bartender, Sam, was still there. Sure enough Sam was there, and he remembered me from the previous visit. Over an ale, we talked about the group from two years before. Sam filled me in on the whereabouts of the various members. Then he told me that Hamid had come back only once and that he was sad because he'd been engaged to be married to a woman he'd met in London. They'd planned to meet in Cyprus, but the woman had stood him up. Oh my God! It didn't take much for me to realize that woman was me!

My mind flew back to that week in London, trying to find anything that would indicate we were engaged. The only thing that came to mind was the necklace he gave me.

Several years later while working in Kuwait, I learned that accepting a gift such as a gold necklace from a man was an invitation for something more. In my case, it meant engaged. My understanding of cultural differences was broadening.

I became a little bit more cautious when I accepted gifts from men, but at the same time, I usually accept all gifts at face value. Personally, I feel a gift doesn't come with attachments, conditions, or expectations. If it does, it's not a gift. I see giving a gift as an offering from the heart of one person to another.

My second betrothal happened in Nigeria.

During one of our shorter holidays, two fellow volunteers and I decided to take a road trip to Jalingo in Taraba State to visit Jack, a veteran CUSO volunteer. Trekking to different states and staying with CUSO members was a great way to see the country and connect with fellow Canadians.

Much of this journey required travelling in overcrowded minivans. It was the end of the hot season, so it was hot and muggy. The humidity was rising and we knew that rain was coming. Being squashed in a minivan with hot, sweaty people for hours was rather uncomfortable.

Then the skies opened up and it began to rain. The minivan stopped, everyone clambered out, and we danced in the rain. We were wet from sweat, so being drenched by rain didn't make any difference. In fact, it was refreshing and exhilarating to dance in the middle of nowhere with a group of happy laughing people. As the rain began to subside, we got back into the bus and carried on to our destination. This little shower cooled the air and made for a more pleasant journey.

We arrived in Jalingo in the early evening, tired and wet. The next morning, we wandered around the town and went to the market to buy food for our communal meals. Laden with our supplies, we returned to Jack's house to visit and play cards, listen to music, cook food, and read books.

Jack had been in Nigeria for four years, so he was a wellseasoned volunteer. It was interesting to be with him because everyone in the town knew him and he had great stories to tell of his life in Nigeria.

Each evening, our little group would head off to the local bush bar. A bush bar was a fancy name for tables and chairs under a couple of trees with Christmas lights (or fairy lights, as the locals called them) strung on branches for light, and with loud music blaring from speakers. This was a place to drink, dance, and meet locals. A woman didn't usually go alone unless she was a lady of the night.

Jack and his friends were our escorts. I love to dance, and before long I was up dancing and laughing with the others. It was a funfilled evening!

Later in the evening, Jack was huddled at the end of the table, deep in conversation with a group of men. Every now and then, they turned and looked at us, then continued talking. My friends and I noticed and wondered what was going on, but mostly we ignored them and carried on talking with the Nigerian ladies. A typical men's group and ladies' group.

As we walked back to the house, Jack looked at me and said, "It's a good thing you are leaving tomorrow." I asked, "Why?" He replied, "I sold you tonight for two cows, six goats, and 10 chickens." I stopped dead in my tracks. "You did what?" He looked at me with a big grin and said, "Yeah, Danjuma really liked you. He said you have good hips and can bring many babies. I knew you were leaving tomorrow, so I thought I would have some fun." As one, my female friends and I stopped and looked at him with disbelief. We then gave him a piece of our minds. He said it was all in fun. We didn't think so.

The next morning, we were back in a minivan heading home. Our conversation turned to the previous night's transaction. I reflected on how I felt from this experience. What surfaced was a deeper understanding of what it felt like for so many girls whose lives were traded for animals. Girls who had no say in these transactions and were expected to do as they were told. I came away with compassion for women who don't have a say in how they lived their lives.

I was grateful to be born in a culture that gave me choices.

In both of these engagements, I got a glimpse of how different my culture was from other cultures. I realized that I knew very little about other cultures and how naive I was. The more I travelled, the more I understood and respected other cultures.

Growing up, we had a wall hanging in our home that said, "Before you judge another, walk a mile in their shoes." Now I knew what that meant.

# Chapter Thirteen
## Personal Space! What Personal Space?

What do you consider reasonable personal space? At what point do you feel uncomfortable or threatened by the proximity of someone else?

Before I left Canada, I never thought much about it. With some people, I stood close, and with others, I stood farther apart. When I stepped off the plane in Nigeria, my cultural perception of personal space got a makeover. It began the first day in Kano Airport, where I stood shoulder to shoulder with fellow passengers as we made our way through the chaos at customs.

Canada has the luxury of wide-open spaces, whereas many of the countries I lived in don't have this luxury. The idea of personal space is non-existent.

In Nigeria, I learned to be comfortable in a crowded taxi, minivan, bus, or boat. I discovered that it was rude to step back when someone came close enough that I could see the pores in their skin. As a result, my personal space shrank. In markets, I became comfortable being surrounded by people inches away. This narrowing of space was a problem when I returned to Canada for visits, having forgotten that Canadians needed more personal space and were often territorial about it.

Living in highly populated countries meant that you could never really be alone, even in what appeared to be a quiet, idyllic spot in nature.

On a Saturday, a group of friends decided to go for a picnic. A small river was several kilometres from our village, and we headed there thinking it would be a quiet place to spend the afternoon. We arrived at a lovely spot beside the river without a soul in sight. We spread out our blankets, and before we had time to turn around, a trickle of people had arrived and sat not far from us. Within five minutes, a crowd had gathered. Tell me, how would you enjoy your picnic lunch when you have 20 or 30 sets of eyes watching you? Luckily, we had plenty of food to share with our audience.

This situation was not unique to Nigeria, for I experienced it in many other countries. In fact, on road trips in Ethiopia, I began to time how long it took before a crowd gathered. As soon as we stopped our vehicle in what appeared to be a non-populated piece of countryside, I started counting. By the time I counted to five, the first group had arrived, and by the time I reached 10, we had a crowd. It never failed.

The examples above were everyday occurrences that eventually became normal. But, three particular occasions left me less than comfortable.

My first solo trip to the bank in Jos, the state capital, left me overwhelmed and confused.

As I stepped across the threshold into the bank, the scene before me was astounding. The bank was full of people, mostly men. When I say the bank was full, I mean wall-to-wall of people. I stood rooted with my back to the door and wondered how I was going to make my way to the counter. All I saw was a mass of individuals jostling to move forward. I'm 5 foot 3 inches tall, and most of the people in front of me were taller. What to do?

Jostling people aside in a crowd went totally against my upbringing and cultural background.

I needed money, so there was no option except to make my way to the counter. Eventually I made my move, trying not to be too pushy and yet wanting to keep moving forward, so I had to be a little aggressive. I nudged my way to the counter with a steady stream of "excuse me, excuse me, excuse me." Finally, I reached a teller, only to discover that I was at the wrong one.

I didn't realize that you handed your cheque to one teller, then stepped away and waited. The first teller processed it and passed it to a second teller, who you picked it up from when your name was called. Yes, one more journey through the sea of people. Then, you made your way through the crowd, once more, to the last teller to get your money.

Two hours later I left the bank with my money, exhausted and not looking forward to the next visit.

I repeated this process for several months until the day that the bank manager noticed me in the crowd. He called me into his office and asked me what I was doing in the country and how come my husband wasn't doing the banking. When he discovered I was a volunteer and single, he invited me to bypass the line. He also suggested that I bring my cheque to him every month. While I did my shopping in the city, he had the cheque cashed, and I picked up the envelope of money from his office on my way out of town. Another gift from the universe landing in my lap!

The experience at the bank paled in comparison to being caught up in a mob as my friends and I attempted to board a ferry.

Three of my fellow female volunteers and I decided to visit southern Nigeria. North, middle, and south Nigeria are very different geographically, economically, and culturally. Two of my friends lived in the northern region, while my other friend and I lived in the middle part of Nigeria. We wanted to see as much of the country as we could during our stay and were happy to have travel companions.

Our journey began in Jos and took us through Lafia, Makurdi, Enugu, and Onitsha, then to our final destination of Calabar. We stopped for a night in Enugu and spent a couple of days in Onitsha to explore one of the largest outdoor market in Nigeria. In this market, you could buy anything! Go ahead, let your imagination run wild.

Eventually we arrived in Calabar, which is nestled in the southeast corner of Nigeria on the shores of the Bight of Biafra. It was hot, humid, crowded, and very different from our regions.

We visited the city sites, canoed through the mangroves, and travelled to a small island to visit a museum.

To get to the island, we took a small local ferry. It was a pleasant ride without the crowds that one usually encountered on public transportation. We made sure that we knew what time the last ferry departed because the hostess of our guest house informed us there were no hotels, and that the island was unsafe at night. We visited the museum, purchased a few snacks for the return ferry ride, and meandered our way to the ferry landing.

We arrived at the landing to see a pushing, shoving, and aggressive mob of people waiting to board the ferry. We froze on the spot. I was terrified of getting near this group, as they were fighting their way through the crowd and jostling each other to get to the front of the line. Right behind that heartpounding fear was the worry of being left on the island.

We were sure we wouldn't get on the ferry because none of us wanted to join that crowd.

At the entrance to the ferry were four police officers shouting and using whips in an attempt to keep the people from charging forward. Much to our surprise, one of the officers shouted to us, saying, "Do you have tickets?" We responded, "Yes, we do." The officers ordered us to come to the ferry. With a deep inhalation and much trepidation, we entered the swarm of people. As we inched our way forward, the police used their bodies to clear a very narrow path for us. At the gate, an officer whisked us onto the ferry, and he stayed near us for the journey back. Even the police didn't stay on the island at night.

It was terrifying to be pressed in from all sides, knowing that if I fell, I wouldn't get up. It was equally horrifying to hear the whips whistle by my ear and over my head. And it was even more horrific to see people beaten because of us. The injustice of it made me feel nauseated. It did make me very aware that when your physical safety and life are in danger, you'll do anything to stay alive. From experience, I know that when you're faced with these extreme situations, a natural survival instinct kicks in. You don't think, you just act.

Behind us the locals poured onto the ferry, filling it to overflowing. The short ride back to the mainland was very different from the ride over.

As the ferry neared the pier, people began to climb out the sides and jump onto the dock. The ferry started to tilt precariously as the passengers migrated to one side of the ferry. There was no waiting for the ferry to dock. We were sitting on the side of the boat where people were exiting, and they were stepping on our laps and shoulders to get out. All we could do was move aside. By now, our police escort disappeared.

We left the ferry feeling shaken. Back at the guest house, each of us collapsed on our bed, exhausted from the emotion that was still flowing through us. We were happy to be alive, but the images of the brutality were seared in our minds.

That was the most terrifying experience I've ever had. I've endured malaria, survived police checks at gunpoint, witnessed a military coup, heard distant gunshots, and survived a mugging at knifepoint, but none of these came near to what I experienced that day in Calabar.

On my last day in Plateau State, Nigeria provided me with one more experience of limited personal space. This experience became an asset when I reached India.

My contract was completed, my backpack was full, and I was off to see the world. I was travelling with Karen, my longtime high school friend. We were on our way to Nairobi, the first stop on our journey eastward. We were flying from Jos to Lagos and then on to Nairobi.

For the first leg of our trip, Peter and Terry, two civil engineers from Shendam, accompanied us. We arrived several hours before our flight to ensure that we got boarding passes. In Nigeria, nothing was guaranteed. We were also concerned about the weather. Because it was the rainy season, flights were often cancelled, which is what happened with the morning flight. As a result, people were hanging around the airport with boarding passes for two different trips, hoping to get on one airplane.

We secured our boarding passes and went to find a drink.

As time inched closer to the scheduled arrival of our flight, I felt the tension in the air rise. Peter said, "Karen, you hold on to Terry's hand and don't let go. Carolynne, you hold onto mine and don't let go." I thought he was being a bit dramatic, but we were close friends and I trusted him.

When the announcement came that the plane was arriving, Peter took hold of my hand, Terry secured Karen's, and we made our way to the boarding gate. When we arrived, there was already a tense, pushy crowd waiting for the gate open, and soon a long, tightly packed queue formed behind us. Everyone wanted to be on that last flight of the day.

When we saw the aircrew arrive at the gate, Peter gave us one more set of instructions: "When the gate opens, hold on tight and RUN to the plane. When we're on the plane, sit in the first empty seat you see and buckle the seat belt. Don't get up for anyone." The tone of his voice was such that I didn't question it. After all, he was a regular passenger on this flight.

When the gate opened, that surge of humanity pushed forward and everyone ran to the plane, up the stairway, and into the cabin. We found a seat, sat down, and buckled up. All assigned seating went out of the window.

I had a seat, I was buckled in, and I wasn't getting up.

Luckily the four of us had window seats, so we didn't have people jumping over us. As I watched passengers clamber over other passengers to get to a seat, I recalled the ferry a few months earlier. When the plane was full, the door was closed, and the plane was airborne.

I was so happy to be with Peter and Terry, for they knew what to do. I can't imagine what it would've been like if Karen and I'd been alone.

As a result of the flight leaving late, the only worrisome part of this experience was that we would miss our connecting flight to Nairobi because we'd still have to navigate the Lagos airport. As it happened, all went well. Before I knew it, I was sipping an ice-cold beer under the thorn tree at the Stanley Hotel.

Nigeria gave me experiences that prepared me for the next 25 years of my life as a modern-day nomad. With this foundation built on the basics of living a simple life, I've been able to adapt and adjust to whatever situation I find myself in. I'm comfortable with the rich and the poor. And I know that it's not things that make life rich.

# Part Two: My Backpack Is My Home


When Karen and I set out for Kenya in 1985, the only fixed destination we had in mind was Kenya and the only time constraint was Karen's one-year sabbatical leave from work. As for me, my destination was east and my timeline was indefinite. I was following that open door that presented itself to me in Kenya the year before. I put all my trust in the Divine Plan and my inner guidance system. I was following my inner spirit with my backpack as my home.

# Chapter Fourteen
# Kenya Revisited

Returning to Kenya in the summer of 1985 was so different from the previous year. This time I was returning as a traveller with the prerequisite backpack, a Lonely Planet travel guide, and no set itinerary – not even a prebooked flight to the next destination. I had a sense of freedom that's difficult to put into words. It was a feeling of being alive, curious, open, and trusting.

I was also travelling with Karen, my long time friend, whom I had travelled with in the past. She was eager to join me when I told her what I wanted to do on completing my contract with CUSO. She was ready to take a break from her corporate job, and they were willing to give her a year's sabbatical. So, in June 1985, she joined me in Nigeria for a few weeks before we embarked on this adventure into the unknown.

Upon our arrival in Nairobi, Karen and I quickly settled into the Nairobi hostel. I was happy to be back and excited to show Karen the sites. In the 1980s, downtown Nairobi was the place to be. There was the market and the Stanley Hotel's Thorn Tree Cafe. There were also bookstores, boutiques, cafés, and shops with a variety of food stuff: all the things I didn't have while I was living in Nigeria.

Naturally, the first place to stop was the Thorn Tree Cafe. After we placed our order of Tusker beer and some food, I wandered over to the traveller's bulletin board on the tree to read the notices. Not surprisingly, I found a few messages from people I met the previous year. The traveller's telegraph was working well.

We hung out in Nairobi for several days as we organized our next adventures. Every morning we took a *matatu*, an overcrowded minibus which was the local form of a transit system, from the hostel to downtown where we proceeded to go to our favourite café for breakfast. Breakfast consisted of freshly brewed Kenyan coffee and food. As you can see, coffee was the top priority. Two years of deprivation, except for the two weeks in Togo, was rewarded with rich, full-bodied Kenya gold.

A safari was at the top our list of things to do. I'd already been to the Masai Mara National Reserve and was keen to return, but I also wanted to see other parks. This was a bit trickier because of our budget constraints.

I was in my glory and happy to be sharing this experience with Karen. Eventually, we booked a camping safari that took us to several game parks: including Amboseli, Meru, Tsavo East and West, and Masai Mara. We ended this expedition in Tsavo West, where I had my first very close encounter with the wildlife. Tsavo National Park, which opened in 1948, is the oldest and largest park in Kenya. Tsavo West is known for its majestic views of Mount Kilimanjaro in Tanzania. I loved waking up just before sunrise and watching the ring of clouds rise until Mount Kilimanjaro came into view, shining with the morning sun.

At the campsite, we pitched our tents under a structure, which consisted of huge wooden poles with a thatched roof, but open on all sides. At previous campsites we put up our tents in the open, and I wondered why this time we set up under the shelter.

After a long day of travel and another wonderful campfire dinner, I crawled into my sleeping bag and quickly fell asleep. Sometime later, I woke up to a loud rustling right beside the tent. I listened to get a feel for how close the sound was and tried to guess who it was. Karen was fast asleep, but I was curious. I wanted to know who or what was making the sound. So, very slowly, I unzipped the tent flap while silently cursing the noise it was making. Ziiiippppp! When it opened enough, I slowly pulled the flap back, cautiously looked out, and saw a huge elephant foot a few feet from my nose. Damn! With one flip, I closed the flap and sat back in amazement. An elephant! It was right outside our tent! Now I knew why we were under the canopy. I sat for a long time and listened while the elephants munched on the vegetation around the shelter. All the while, I hoped that the baby elephants stayed close to their mamas and didn't venture under the roof of the shelter and onto our tents. The elephant stayed there for about an hour before moving off, and that's when I went back to sleep.

The next morning at breakfast, I shared my story with the group. Our guide had a good laugh, but Karen wasn't very amused.

When it comes to nature, I have a natural curiosity, which was encouraged by my dad. He always took the time to answer my questions and explain things to me. Besides, I'd rather know what I was facing than sit in fear of an imaginary visitor.

After camping for 10 days, we returned to the city feeling content, needing a long, hot shower, and requiring clean clothes. I was well trained in hand washing clothes. Thank you, Shendam!

After spending a few days in Nairobi, we prepared for our next destination: Mombasa. We could get there by bus, train, or airplane. Flying was out of the question for us budget travellers. The other choices were an overcrowded bus or a historical overnight train ride. It wasn't really a choice.

I love travelling by car, bus, train, boat, or ferry. Any means of travelling on land is preferable because I love to see the people and the places of the area I'm travelling through. Air travel is OK for long distances, but it always feels like I'm missing out on what is on the ground.

The overnight train from Nairobi to Mombasa is one of the most epic train journeys in Africa, starting from Mombasa and going into Uganda. The rail line is over 100 years old. I feel so grateful to have had three return trips on this train.

We started our journey at the Nairobi train station.

Karen and I found our second-class compartment and boarded the train. You could buy three classes of tickets: first, second, and third. The main difference between first and second class was that first class was a private compartment for two people, while second class had four bunks. Third class didn't have compartments; the seats were often overcrowded and you had to sit up all night. Most travellers at that time chose second class. It was a great way to meet people, swap stories, get recommendations, and hear warnings of places or things to avoid.

The train usually left in the late afternoon and arrived in Mombasa in the early morning. Once we were settled in and introduced ourselves to other travellers, we shared food and ordered drinks from the porter. The view as we left Nairobi was one of shanties on the border of the city. As the sun set, the conversation flowed and the card games began. Around 9 p.m., the porter came to drop down the top bunk and make the beds for the night.

Having grown up as a railway worker's daughter, I was well versed with the sway and rocking of a train and how it lulls you to sleep. I elected to sleep on the top bunk, and as soon as the lights went out I was fast asleep.

I woke up in the early dawn and gazed out the window at the African savannah passing by. As the train traversed through Tsavo National Park, I saw herds of antelopes and wildebeests, dazzles of zebras, and a sounder of wild boar in the distance. On other trips I saw elephants and giraffes. At each village, children would run alongside the train waving at the passengers, who would often toss candy or chewing gum to them.

Around 7:30 a.m., the porters gathered the bedding, lifted up the upper bunk so we could sit, and later, returned with breakfast. If I recall correctly, it was tea with milk, a left over from the British colonial days, a boiled egg, and toast. No coffee! The further east we travelled, the less coffee was available. Breakfast done, the porters took the trays and the outskirts of Mombasa came into view.

Our visit was just long enough to visit Fort Jesus, to photograph the famous tusks commemorating Queen Elizabeth's visit in 1952, and to find the bus going to the island of Lamu. The beach was calling.

In 1985, the only way to reach the island by land was by going on a bone-jarring, full day journey on a dilapidated bus, and then taking a short ferry ride from the old town of Lamu to the island.

Oh, but it was so worth the effort.

When we arrived in Lamu, the only accommodation options were one small luxury hotel, a few hostels, and bed rentals on several families' flat rooftops. A bed, or really a canvas cot, cost the equivalent of about five dollars a night. Karen and I opted for a rooftop bed, sharing the space with four other travellers. It was absolutely amazing to lie in bed under a canopy of stars each night and listen to the gentle rhythm of the waves.

In addition to providing the beds on the rooftop, our host family also created a shaded area for us with a large woven mat, cushions, and pillows. Tea was readily available all day long. Although Lamu was very safe in those days, we placed all our valuables in a safe in the main house. No one locked their doors on the island. Lamu had virtually no crime, as Arabic law can be very harsh. We were considered honoured guests in their house and were treated as such. Within a couple days, we became part of the family.

Lamu was my first taste of Arab culture. The hospitality, acceptance, and generosity I felt was heartwarming. The town was characterized by narrow streets and magnificent stone buildings with impressive curved doors, and influenced by a unique fusion of Swahili, Arabic, and Persian cultures. I loved wandering down the streets and admiring the beautifully carved wooden doors, knowing that behind each door was a courtyard garden surrounded by living quarters.

We spent most of our days lounging on white sandy beaches and swimming in the clear waters of the Indian Ocean. Before long, we became friends with the other travellers. Only hardy individuals made the journey, so there were few of us. We had impromptu concerts on rooftops where we sang and danced. On occasion, we held potluck dinners where we pooled our resources, dinners where I was introduced to Arabic and Indian cuisine. No one seemed to mind that this was a dry island (no alcohol). It was paradise!

All good things come to an end. After a few weeks of enjoying the beach, it was time to move on. We had one more area of Kenya to see before we moved on to explore the rest of the world.

We made our way back the same way we came: the jarring bus ride to Mombasa, then the train back to Nairobi. After spending a few days in Nairobi, we boarded another train, this time heading west to Kisumu on the shores of Lake Victoria. It was a scenic journey through the Great Rift Valley and into the lush forest around Lake Victoria.

This was a different train ride, as we were seated in second class with no berths (beds), and our travelling companions were mainly Kenyans. Most travellers didn't venture this way. Personally, I wanted to set my toe in Lake Victoria, the largest lake in Africa and the second largest in the world after Lake Superior in Canada. That's as far as we could safely go, as we were advised not to enter Uganda because of the unrest caused by Idi Amin's expulsion.

Kisumu and Lake Victoria were anticlimatic after all of our other adventures in Kenya, so after a couple of days we returned to Nairobi.

Our last days in Kenya were occupied with getting visas for Egypt and India, as well as flights to Cairo. Fellow travellers had warned us to get our India visa in Kenya, as it was easier to get it there than it would be in Egypt. Although we had the traveller's bible, the *Lonely Planet* guide, word of mouth was the most up-to-date and reliable information, especially when it came from several sources.

Pyramids were the next thing on our list!

# Chapter Fifteen
## Wandering the Streets of Cairo

Karen and I arrived in Cairo in the early afternoon. We found a taxi, negotiated the fare, and headed to the budget accommodations. How did we know where to go, you ask?

Before arriving in Cairo, we consulted our travel guide and made a list of the top four guest houses that appealed to us. When it came to budget travelling, we always wanted to ensure that the accommodations had available rooms (remember, this was pre-Internet), that the place was clean, and that the people were friendly. And, for me, it had to feel right! I'd walk into a place, and if the vibes weren't right, I wouldn't stay. Fortunately, Karen had known me for many years and trusted my instinct. She often waited on the street with both our backpacks while I raced up the stairs to check out the hostel or guest house. If it was a thumbs down, we went looking for the next place on our list.

The guest house we selected in Cairo was a lovely place owned and operated by a wonderful woman who spoke several languages. She was a wealth of information and our cultural advisor. Each day as we ate breakfast, she'd review our plans and give us suggestions for how to get where we wanted to go, as well as inform us of the dos and don'ts for two single women wandering around in a Muslim country. At the end of each day, we'd come back to the guest house and share our adventures with her. It was like having an elder sister watching over us.

Our guest house was near Tahrir Square in the heart of Cairo and within easy walking distance to many of the sites. Of course, at the top of our list was a visit to the Pyramids of Giza. With explicit instructions from our host, we managed to make our way to and from the pyramids by city bus.

In the mid-1980s, there were no lineups or crowds. As we meandered around and through the pyramids, we'd only occasionally come across small groups of tourists. Sometimes we'd stand behind a group of English-speaking tourists and listen to the guide talk about that particular part of the pyramid, but mostly we explored the pyramids on our own. It was great because we could spend as much time as we wanted in different areas. We were able to sit on the floor, close our eyes, and feel the energy without being disturbed.

After several hours going through the pyramids, I recall that I felt puzzled because I didn't feel a sense of "wow". I think I expected something more. Instead, I came away feeling a little disappointed. Over the years, I learned that exceptions rarely match up to reality; therefore, now I go with no expectations and stay open to what shows up.

The Egyptian Museum, on the other hand, blew my mind. The staggering collection of antiquities displayed in Cairo's Egyptian Museum was overwhelming. It was huge, with a jumble of artifacts crammed into every available space. We stood at the entrance with our museum-provided map and our tickets in an attempt to strategically plan our viewing route. In the end, we gave up and headed to the Tutankhamun galleries. If you haven't seen the live exhibit, then my words won't do it justice. It was magnificent! I must admit that the rest of the museum paled in comparison, although we went to the museum twice and still didn't see all of it. I've heard that the new museum is beautiful and well laid out. Perhaps it warrants a visit.

Another day, we made our way to the Al Azhar Mosque, one of the city's earliest surviving mosques. To balance things out, we wandered the streets of Old Cairo. This area is rich in history. I loved wandering through the narrow streets filled with life and vibrancy, wondering what it was like before cars and modern conveniences.

A visit to Khan el Khalili, the primary market or *souk* in Cairo, was like stepping back in time. Its labyrinthine skinny alleyways were lined with a huge variety of items, such as spices, food, cloth, carpets, and gold and silver jewelry.

I thought the markets in Nigeria were great, but this vast *souk* was clean, colourful, enticing, and friendly. No massive crowds of people jostled you. We strolled throughout the *souk* as our eyes took in the kaleidoscope of impressions. I had to keep reminding myself that if something I wanted didn't fit in the backpack, I couldn't have it. So, I settled for a cup of Arabic coffee, a few dates, and some sweet, syrupy pastries.

After several days of walking past the perfume shops, we decided to venture in and explore. These weren't perfumes as we know them; instead, they were naturally extracted flower essences. The major perfume manufacturers from France purchased many of these fragrances.

The moment we stepped over the threshold into the shop, the shopkeeper invited us to sit down, and within minutes he placed a steaming cup of tea before us. He proceeded to elaborately explain the different essences to us in perfect English. As he described the various scents, he would dab a little of the oil on the back of our hand, the palm of our hand, our wrist, our arm, or behind our ears until we could no longer differentiate between all the different scents.

However, when he suggested putting a drop of essence on our ankles, we knew it was time to put a stop to the testing. We each made a small purchase and departed with a smile. We smelled like a flower garden as we walked down the street to the guest house. Over our evening tea, we shared our tale with our hostess, who shook her head and laughed with us.

For several days we wandered the streets of Cairo, not always with a destination in mind. As a result, we found ourselves in the surrounding neighbourhoods, where the local people would smile and greet us. When we were in Kenya, we heard some horror stories of men hassling women, but we never had a problem. It could've been because we were in our 30s and older than most other travellers, or it may have been the sage advice our hostess gave us about clothing and greetings. I'm sure that my training at the University of Nigeria also helped. It was while I was there that I learned to dress modestly, preferably in a dress or a skirt that went down the midcalf, and to show no cleavage and cover my shoulders.

On one of our walks, we found ourselves in the City of the Dead, a UNESCO World Heritage site consisting of a series of vast Islamic-era necropolises and cemeteries. It wasn't one of the destinations on our to-do list, but it was fascinating. Karen and I had no had a problem with cemeteries. We enjoyed looking at the dates on the headstones. The mausoleums were intricately carved and gorgeous. As we walked, gawking around, we noticed that people were living in some of the mausoleums. It was shocking, but neither Karen and I nor the people were afraid; instead, we were curious about one another. They may not have ever seen two White Western women walking through there before, and we didn't expect to see families living there. We smiled, they smiled, and we kept on going.

Later on while reading our guide book, we discovered that over the years, people resorted to squatting within the mausoleums and tomb enclosures, turning them into improvised housing. In Canada, we take so much for granted and this accidental (or perhaps not so accidental) visit to the City of the Dead gave me a deeper appreciation of my privileged life. I was on a world adventure, while these families barely eked out a living. What a contrast!

After a week in Cairo, we boarded the day train for Luxor. We reserved first-class seats and were impressed by the whole experience. This train runs along the Nile. Out of the window to the east was desert. To the west was verdant farmland, palm trees, mudbrick houses, and beyond, towering sandy cliffs as the train headed south to Upper Egypt.

If the pyramids didn't impress me, Luxor did. Luxor was small, peaceful, and quiet, especially after Cairo. It's on the site of ancient Thebes and the home of the Karnak Temple with its massive pillars and hieroglyphics.

I was mesmerized as I walked through the temple. It was so beautiful! My head was tilted upward, a smile was on my face, wonder was in my heart, and my mind was full of imagination. Here was the ancient Egypt I'd read about as a child.

West across the Nile is the Valley of Kings, which hosts the tomb of Tutankhamun, the Valley of the Queens, and the Colossi of Memnon.

To see these sites, we had to go on a tour. It was worth it. I have to admit that I've never been very good on tours, as I like to spend more time in some places and want to zip through others. As a history major, I knew I could read about the site if I wanted to know the details. I liked to feel places, to be quiet, and to notice what arose.

When I'm on a tour, I'm either way behind or way ahead of the group. I try not to disrupt the guide or the group. I sense things, see things, and know things that don't always make it into history books. These sites had a heaviness that wasn't on the other side of the river in Luxor.

One of my lasting memories is of a late afternoon and early evening cruise on the Nile in a *felucca*, a traditional Egyptian sailboat. It was peaceful and calm as we caught the wind moving through the Nile. It was one of those pinch-me moments. I was sailing on the Nile!

# Chapter Sixteen
# I Don't Think We Should Be Here!

Egypt is more than just pyramids, hieroglyphics, and tombs. Karen and I were saturated from a two-week diet of ancient Egypt, and we were ready for some relaxation. We headed to the beach. Sharm El Sheik, our destination, is located on the southern tip of the Sinai Desert on the shores of the Red Sea.

In 1985, Sharm El Sheik was a small village and had only one resort hotel, which was out of our budget.

The only alternative accommodation was a tent on the beach in the sand. After all, we were in a desert. An enterprising family had set up a string of tents with cots and lawn chairs, then rented them out to people like us. Some other locals owned a beach restaurant, and a third group rented out snorkel equipment. Being adventurous and wanting some beach time, we figured this was a great deal. Dollarwise, it was prefect!

We forgot to factor in the daytime heat! The daytime temperature hovered around 35C degrees, and our only shade was the tent or the awning at the restaurant. We weren't in an oasis with palm trees but in the desert, raw and bare. The first couple of days weren't too bad because we rented snorkel equipment and spent hours in the water.

The Red Sea is a great place for snorkelling. The corals are some of the most beautiful in the world. The sea life was so abundant and colourful that we spent hours floating around the coral walls. We swam with octopuses, turtles, and an array of sea life. It was hard to stop and get out of the water.

While in the water, we could forget about the heat and sand onshore. When we emerged from the water the heat hit us, and we had few places to hide. Fortunately, when the sun set for the night, the desert cooled and the nights were pleasant.

Other than snorkelling and reading in the shade of our tent, there was little to do. After several days of snorkelling, we were ready to resume sightseeing. We had one more area to explore before our visa expired.

We rode the bus back to Cairo, then took the train to Alexandria.

Founded by Alexander the Great, Alexandria held a fascination for me.

t's a city with ancient sites, along with the famous library. The Library of Alexandria filled my imagination with questions of what knowledge and information we lost when it was destroyed.

Over a few days, we visited sites such as the Citadel of Qaitbay, Montaza Palace, Roman Amphitheatre of Alexandria, Alexandria National Museum, Ras El Tin Palace, and the Catacombs of Kom El Shoqafa. On our list, we dutifully checked off the places we'd seen; however, one place remained.

On our last day in Alexandria, we set off for what we thought would be a short walk to see the Serapeum of Saqqara and Pompey's Pillar. We had our city map with street names written in Arabic that so far had helped us to navigate with ease. As we walked, we often stopped to check that the street name corresponded to our map. It took a bit of deciphering to make sure the squiggle on the street sign matched the squiggle on the map.

At one point, we began to sense that perhaps we weren't heading in the right direction. We stopped under a street sign to figure out where we were. We must've looked strange, standing there with our heads bobbing up and down. I don't recall how long we stood there, but it must've been a while. With some trepidation, we started to realize that we didn't know where we were. We didn't even know which way to go to return to our guest house.

While our heads were bent down over the map, we heard a man's voice. We looked up to see an elderly gentleman standing beside us. He smiled, and after we greeted one another, he pointed to the map and spoke in Arabic. We quickly realized he was asking us where we wanted to go. We pointed to the spot on the map, and he indicated we should wait. He yelled something, and before long a young boy came running towards us. The man said something to the boy, who turned, started to walk away, and waved at us to follow him. We looked at the older man. He smiled, nodded his head in agreement, and gestured for us to follow the boy.

With complete trust, we scampered after the young lad. We walked down the street, which led to a narrower street, which led to a lane, which led to a path. The path, much like a goat trail, wandered up the side of a hill. I looked at Karen and she looked at me, each of us knowing what the other was thinking: "I don't think we should be here." But, we were lost, we were afraid, and we had no option but to follow the boy.

As we climbed the hill, women with their children stared at us as they came out of caves dug into the hills. The young boy greeted the ladies; we smiled and nodded our heads in a greeting. More ladies came out of these caves. They smiled, then laughed and waved at us.

The fear began to subside. I can recall thinking about the money belt I had strapped to my waist containing my passport, money, and credit cards. I also wondered where the heck we were going. In the end, I let myself trust that everything would be OK. I returned the smiles and waves and kept walking.

About 20 minutes later, we emerged onto a street, turned a corner, and stopped. With a big grin, our young guide pointed at the structure before us: Pompey's Pillar. We gave him some money and thanked him. He shook our hands and scampered away.

Karen and I stood gazing up at the pillar, wondering about the risk we took to see this enormous piece of rock.

Trust is powerful energy. I didn't realize it until much later in life, but trust carries a vibration that others feel. That moment when Karen and I looked at each other and gave into complete trust, the energy around us changed.

When we returned to Cairo and shared our adventure with our hostess, she went silent. She looked at us, shook her head, and then told us we'd walked through an area known to the Egyptians as the Den of Thieves.

I don't believe in life lessons. I do believe in life experiences and insights gained from them. Insight is more about wisdom than a lesson learned. Lessons carry the connotation of right and wrong, whereas wisdom indicates something gained and is neither right nor wrong. What happened was what happened, nothing more and nothing less.

# Chapter Seventeen
## The Road Less Travelled

The first time I read Robert Frost's poem, *"The Road Not Taken"*, the words resonated with me. At some deeper level, I knew I didn't want to follow the path that everyone else was following. I wanted more from life. I felt the pull to explore the world that most people shied away from. I wanted to feel the pulse of the people living in the places I visited.

In the mid-1980s, India wasn't at the top of the list for most tourists. It was a popular destination for spiritual seekers and budget travellers. Karen and I fell into the second category. We were there to see and experience this ancient land.

We began our adventures in Delhi in mid-September. True to the pull of the road less travelled, I wanted to visit Srinagar high in the Himalayas before winter. I was fascinated by its Mogul and British history. The other pull was the Himalayas. I can't really explain this affinity. Mountains make my heart soar and give me a deep feeling of inner peace, like I'm closer to source.

The Taj Mahal and the rest of India would have to wait.

We chose to travel to Srinagar by bus, probably because it was the most cost-efficient mode of transportation. Out of all the bus journeys I've been on, that bus trip was the most challenging.

It was a 48-hour journey on a crowded local bus that played non-stop Bollywood movies. The driver insisted we sit in the two front seats beside the door, which was right in front of the TV. It wasn't long before we realized the gift we were given. The seats were hard and uncomfortable, but we had a little more leg room. Plus, the stench on the bus could be overwhelming, and this location was a small mercy. If we'd sat further back in the bus, it would've been hot, crowded, smelly, and probably unsafe. Two women travelling alone on a local bus, I learned later from an Indian friend, targeted them for inappropriate advance or harassment.

The bus frequently stopped at rest stops. There, we could stretch our legs, get fresh air, use the washroom, if we dared, and buy food and drinks, which we avoided. We quickly realized that it was wise to eat very little and sip water sparingly so that we wouldn't need to use the rest stop's bathroom facilities. I thought I'd seen the worst restrooms in Africa, but

India's rest stops won the prize.

The scenery was spectacular once we reached the foothills and climbed higher and higher into the Himalayas. In the terraced fields, families were harvesting grain and vegetables. Onions, chilies, garlic, and other vegetables were laid out on the flat rooftops to dry. Cows, goats, yaks, and donkeys grazed contentedly in the fields. It was easy to ignore the crowded, smelly bus when there were so many astounding things to see.

When we arrived in Srinagar after dark, we were grateful we'd prebooked two nights on a houseboat. One of the main draws to Srinagar was the post-British Raj houseboats that dotted Dal Lake's edges.

The owner of the houseboat met us at the bus station and took us to the boat. Right away I had an uneasy feeling, but it was night and we needed a place to stay. Shortly after we arrived, we ate a meal of rice and dal. It was great to have a warm meal and a hot cup of chai after hours of very little food. It was also cold and damp in the houseboat, which had no heating. My body, used to African heat, wasn't happy.

Once the houseboat owner left, we put on our pyjamas and crawled into bed, vowing to find another place to stay the next day. We were exhausted from our marathon bus ride and immediately fell asleep under a pile of blankets.

The next morning over breakfast, the houseboat owner began to pester us into extending our stay. We were evasive; even though we knew we'd be looking for another houseboat during the day, it didn't feel right to let him know.

After breakfast, we arranged for a *shikara*, a gondola-style water taxi, to take us to Old Delhi so we could explore. Abdul, our *shikara* driver, was a young boy about 14 years old who spoke good English. During our conversation, we mentioned we wanted to find another place to stay. He said he knew of a place and would take us after visiting the *souk* (market).

We wandered around Old Delhi, checked out the *souk*, bought some goodies, and then went back to the landing. As promised, Abdul was waiting for us. He took us to a beautiful large, bright houseboat, where we were greeted by an older man with a warm smile that lit up his eyes and face. He introduced himself as Mohan, and then proceeded to show us around the boat. He informed us that his family had been part of this boat for three generations. The British family who owned this boat during India's British rule had employed his grandparents and parents. When the British family left India, they gave the boat to his family.

The decision was made; we were going to move in the next day. On the *shikara* ride back to the other boat, Abdul, who would be our guide for our stay in Srinagar, informed us that it would be best not to tell the first boat owner where we were moving, as there was some rivalry between houseboat owners. My intuition that had guided me not to speak up in the morning was validated.

Now came the dilemma of what to tell the houseboat owner. I can't remember what we said, but he wasn't happy.

The next morning, right on cue, Abdul arrived to take us to our newfound home. Once again, Mohan greeted us with warm smiles and gave each of us a cup of chai.

Our new room was a large suite with its own bathroom and stove. Luxury for a few dollars a night!

With Mohan's guidance, we took day trips to various parts of the valley.

The first trip was to Gulmarg, a glacier with amazing views of the Himalayas. The most astonishing sight was the men and women slipping and sliding on the glacier ice in their flip-flops. They were having such a wonderful time trying to walk on the ice without falling. Their laughter was infectious. It may have appeared silly to us Canadians, but they were having a blast, and we couldn't help but smile.

We took trips to a couple of famous hill stations. The British developed most of India's hill stations to get respite from the oppressive summer heat. We visited Pahalgam, and Sonmarg.

I was surprised by the fields of fall crocuses. A bigger surprise was that saffron comes from the crocus. Workers pick each flower carefully by hand in order not to dislodge the crimson stigma and styles, called threads. This makes saffron one of the most expensive spices in the world. Having seen how it's harvested, I no longer complain about the price.

Along the way, we visited a village famous for its handmade cricket bats, made from a solid piece of wood. Cricket players from around the world came here to have bats crafted specifically to their specifications.

These valleys abounded in fruit trees. We saw apricots, plums, pears, and apple rings spread out on tarps and drying under the sun. Knowing that we had another long bus ride back to Delhi, we purchased a 2 kg bag of dried apricots. This fruit served us well on long bus and train journeys as we explored India.

While in Srinagar, Abdul ferried us to the Shalimar Bagh, the largest Mughal garden in the Kashmir Valley. These gardens have a Persian influence.

Within the garden is a three-terraced garden with a natural spring. Even during autumn, the gardens were a beautiful, peaceful place to spend an afternoon. At night, the garden's oil lamps, called *chini khanas*, are lit. Abdul took us over one night to see the lights. The reflection of the lights on the lake was stunning.

One afternoon, our host Mohan arranged to have a gem merchant come to the house-boat to show us gems. Not only did the gem merchant show us gems such as rubies, emeralds, amethysts, and sapphires, but we also learned how to tell the difference between a fake gem and a real gem. For several hours, we drank tea and learned about gems. Naturally, I purchased a few small emeralds that afternoon.

We visited a carpet factory that made the most beautiful carpets. I learned the differences between a cheap carpet and an expensive carpet through factors like thread count, pattern, and material.

Guess which ones I was drawn to?

The day before we left Srinagar, Abdul invited us to his house to meet his mother. I expected us to go to one of the wooden houses lining Dal Lake. Instead, we made our way down one of the tiny tributaries draining into the lake. We arrived at the little island with a small makeshift hut made out of scrap wood and corrugated iron. In front of this hut was a beautiful woman squatting in front of a small open fire making tea. She looked up at us with a warm, welcoming smile. We got out of the boat, and Abdul introduced us to his mother. She gestured for us to sit on a piece of cloth on the ground and then poured us some chai. With her son interpreting, she thanked us for hiring her son during our stay in the valley. She also was grateful for the socks, gloves, scarves, sweaters, and hats we gave him. In exchange, we thanked her for raising a beautiful son, for being hospitable, and for providing delicious tea.

That moment, sitting there in that humbling environment, is one of my most precious memories of my time in India. No human-made structure can compare to the heart-to-heart connection between people.

It's these roads less travelled that have made all the difference in my life! I've sat with the very rich and the very poor and have never felt inferior or superior to either.

# Chapter Eighteen
## The Ups and Downs of a Shoestring Budget

Travelling on a shoestring budget had its ups and downs. Karen and I made each decision with two things in mind. The first was how much something would cost. As travellers, we always wanted to do as much as possible for as little money as possible. Sometimes things worked out very well and other times they didn't.

The other consideration was the length of our tourist visas. This involved knowing where we had to go to extend the visas or making sure we had a flight out before our visas expired.

As a result of these two considerations, some planning was involved. We made a list of our must-see places and then plotted the route we'd like to go from destination to destination and the means of transportation between the sites. Our calculations also had to take into consideration unforeseen circumstances.

We spent more time in Srinagar than we'd originally planned, but it was so worth it. When we returned to New Delhi, we began putting into motion the next leg of our journey to Rajasthan. We'd be travelling by train, which involved a few trips to the train station to look at schedules and purchase tickets.

Some personal matters required attention, such as collecting our mail at the American Express office and doing our laundry. We also spent a few hours in our favourite coffee shop in Connaught Circle responding to our letters. No computers, cell phones, or Internet existed; all correspondence took place via snail mail.

I loved writing letters home, trying to put into words the sites, sounds, smells, and chaos of India. It was difficult to describe the drivers who constantly blared their car horn, the cows who wandered around, and the negotiation of meager fares with rickshaw drivers. It was tricky to write about beggars of every description, smells of food mixed with urine, throngs of people milling around, and tastes of food that didn't appeal to our taste buds. If you haven't been to India, my descriptions pale compared to the experience. Even after two years of living in Nigeria, India took some getting used to.

After a couple of days' rest, we boarded the train for Jaipur. We opted for a second-class sleeper in a woman's compartment. Having a private compartment was a luxury! The compartment had four bunks, which we shared with two other women. The journey was comfortable, pleasant, and uneventful.

The next morning, we arrived in the pink city of Jaipur. It's the capital of Rajasthan state.

It was a clean, colourful city with beautiful architecture and rich history. In the '80s, it was a lovely city to wander in with its markets, jewelry shops, and textiles. After the noise and bustle of Delhi, it was refreshing.

My most memorable site was the Hawa Mahal. This beautiful, ornate, sandstone building has hundreds of windows previously used by the royal ladies to gaze out at the street life. In the past, royalty, especially the women, were secluded from the outside world.

We also visited the City Palace, Amer Fort, Jantar Manter, an astronomical observatory and Jal Mahal, a water palace sitting in the middle of a lake. Jaipur was a feast for the senses as well as for the imagination.

From Jaipur, we took a train to Udaipur. Unbeknownst to us, we arrived on Diwali's eve, the Festival of Lights, and one of the most popular festivals in India.

As soon as we stepped out of the train station, we were surrounded by rickshaw *wahalla's* (drivers) wanting to take us to various guest houses. Guest house owners gave rickshaw drivers a commission for bringing them guests, so the drivers were quite pushy. They'd often tell you that a particular guest house was closed or full, or they'd flatly refuse to take you. If they refused to take you, that meant they wouldn't get a commission.

As usual, we had a list of guest houses where we wanted to stay, but we soon realized this could be a problem because of the festival. Even though we knew it wouldn't be easy, we insisted on going to the guest houses on our list. After being turned away from the first three on our list, we got lucky with the fourth one.

We settled in and were very pleased to discover that this guest house also served vegetarian meals. The owners served us a traditional *Thali*, which is a plate with a selection of different foods that complement each other so the meal is balanced. We weren't vegetarian, but we did enjoy these meals. By this time, we were tired and in need of a shower and some food. After we ate we headed to our room, thinking we'd get a good night's sleep. Not so!

We barely got tucked into bed when the fireworks began right outside our window. The festival had begun in earnest, and there'd be little sleep for the next five days. After this experience, we always made sure to check our *Lonely Planet* guide for local holidays.

One afternoon, dressed in our finest, we took a boat to the Taj Lake Palace, a five-star luxury hotel located in the middle of Lake Pichola. This hotel was made famous in the James Bond movie *Octopussy*. We walked around the hotel admiring the views of Udaipur. We even splurged and enjoyed a cold beer on the terrace.

As a result of the festival and the hordes of visitors to Udaipur, we saw very little of the city. Instead, we spent five days enjoying Diwali's festivities with some of the other guests at our guest house. If the whole city is partying, you might as well relax and join the festivities.

Our next stop was Jodhpur, which was famous for its blue laneways and buildings. Our main purpose for stopping in Jodhpur was to make a train connection for the next leg of our journey. While there, we visited Mehrangarh Fort and Jaswant Thada, the white marble cenotaphs dedicated to the royals.

We arrived early in the morning and headed straight to the fort. We wandered around the fort and the cenotaphs for several hours. By midday, we were exhausted because we were carrying our backpacks and hadn't taken that into consideration. We had the afternoon to kill as the train didn't leave for Jaisalmer until late afternoon.

We consulted our guidebook and found the cheapest room to rent for the afternoon. It was perfect! It was a tiny room on the second floor of a guest house with one single bed and a washroom down the hall. It was nothing fancy! We were able to set down our backpacks, have a shower, and enjoy an afternoon siesta before heading back to the train station.

The next morning we arrived in Jaisalmer. The Golden City, as Jaisalmer is called, is situated on the edge of the Thar Desert. Much of Jaisalmer is built from sandstone. The fort rises like a sandcastle out of the desert.

Many people live within the fort, and we found a lovely guest house tucked away in one of its corners. Within the fort are seven interconnected Jain temples, and these temples date back to the 15th and 16th centuries.

Jainism is an Indian religion that practices non-injury to any living creature.

While walking through the city, we saw people wearing masks in order to prevent themselves from breathing in insects. They were also very cautious about where they placed their feet, making sure not to step on any living thing. I found it fascinating to sit and watch the people going in and out of the temples. It was so different from anything I'd seen before.

After a couple of days exploring the city, we were ready for another adventure. Our next adventure was a camel safari into the Thar Desert. Our dilemma was the length of the safari. There were several options, but in the end we settled on a two-day and one-night safari. We booked our safari, stored our backpacks at the guest house, packed a small bag of essentials, and searched for our camels.

Several other travellers joined us, and once introductions were done, we climbed onto our camels and headed off into the desert. We started at a nice slow pace to get used to the camels, but later we were trotting for a while and even engaged in a friendly camel race.

Our first stop was the Bada Bagh, a garden complex with cenotaphs erected in honour of the city's royal rulers. It was eerie, yet its exquisite architecture made it an interesting place to investigate.

We rode on for the rest of the afternoon and eventually stopped for the night. We camped outside under the stars. Our guides lit a fire and prepared our evening meal while the rest of us chatted and shared travel stories. After dinner, one of the Israeli members of our group began to sing. As he sang, he encouraged us to get up and dance. Before long, the whole group was singing, clapping, laughing, and dancing around a fire. It was a beautiful starlit evening in the open desert.

The next morning after breakfast, we headed back to Jaisalmer. As we approached the city from the desert, the fort was like a golden sandcastle floating in the air.

We got back to our guest house to find that it was quite full, and there was only one room available. It didn't take us long to find out why this room was empty: rats came in through a hole in the wall.

Karen and I must've looked ridiculous as we sat on the bed with our feet curled up under us, contemplating what we could put in the hole to keep the rats out. Eventually, we got brave enough to get off the bed and slowly inched towards the hole, then stuffed one of our scrunched-up shawls into the opening. Then, we pushed one of our backpacks up against the plugged hole to ensure that the rats wouldn't pop the shawl back out. Needless to say, neither of us had a good sleep that night.

Two days later, we were back in a private compartment on a train to Delhi.

Instead of being a tourist, being a traveller took some getting used to, just like any other major adjustments in life. The moment I stepped out of what was usual or expected, I entered a new heightened awareness as I took in all the nuances of what was happening around me. Constant adjustments to my held patterns and beliefs were required as I navigated situations I'd never experienced before. Some adjustments were smooth and easy, and others were shocking and difficult. Overall, I began to see and admire the resiliency of the human spirit.

# Chapter Nineteen
# Tombs, Temples, and People

The Taj Mahal!

I bet you're thinking, "How come you didn't go there first?" Am I right? As you probably noticed by now, I don't do things the way most people do.

Karen and I arrived in Agra, settled into our guest house, and prepared to explore. No, we didn't make a beeline to the Taj Mahal. Instead, we began our explorations with the Baby Taj, also known as the Itmadud Daulah Tomb. The Baby Taj is a smaller version of the Taj Mahal, and is completely symmetrical.

From there, we wandered around the Mehtab Bagh, a beautiful garden with a breathtaking view of the Taj Mahal across the river.

The Taj Mahal was beckoning!

Our daily guide was the rickshaw driver that we met outside our guest house the day we arrived. Each morning, he greeted us with a big smile, ready to take us anywhere we wanted to go. The following day, he was ready to take us to the Taj Mahal.

I can honestly say that this was one of the most beautiful human-made structures I've seen. At the time of our visit pollution wasn't so bad, and the pristine white marble glittered in the sunlight. I was spellbound when we were inside the Taj, with its jewel-encrusted walls, detailed latticework, and unique architecture. As if that wasn't enough, the next day we returned to view the Taj Mahal glistening under a full moon. That experience was magical.

In addition to the Taj, we spent time at the Red Fort with its impressive history and the Tomb of Akbar the Great.

In 1985, Agra was a small city easy to explore. Even though we weren't into shopping, we didn't escape being sucked into the local shops.

All tourists love to shop, right? This is something that every one of the rickshaw drivers knew. As a result, we were constantly bombarded with our driver's suggestions to take us to jewelry, carpet, or trinket shops. For a few days we evaded his suggestions, but then he became frustrated because the commission from the shops made up a large part of his income.

Finally, we caved. Karen and I were drawn to the carpet shops and agreed to go to one. It was an amazing experience! The owner greeted us at the doorway, ushered us in like royalty, and invited us to sit on a sofa. Refreshments arrived in the form of sweets and chai. Then the show began. The owner proceeded to unfurl carpet after carpet before us. With each one, he explained the intricacies of the weave, material, and design. We soon became overwhelmed with choice.

I knew I wasn't going to buy one because it wouldn't fit in my backpack. Karen, however, wanted one for her living room. She had a house in Canada and I had a backpack. After a second visit to the showroom, Karen bought a carpet and arranged to have it shipped to Canada. Karen got a beautiful carpet, and our rickshaw driver earned his commission as well as a large tip from us.

It was time to move on. Our next destination, Khajuraho, had us up before dawn to catch a local bus to the nearest railway station. We arrived at the station mid-morning, bought a ticket, then waited on the station platform for the train to arrive. There wasn't another traveller or tourist in sight. As we sat on the platform reading our books, a small gathering of locals formed a circle and stared at us. We smiled and they smiled, but we had no other common language. I would've loved to have had a conversation with them, for I was as curious about them as they were about us.

A short train ride brought us to our destination at Khajuraho Junction, where another bus took us to Khajuraho. It was a dawn to dusk journey. I've heard that there are now express trains and taxis to ease the trip, but that also means more tourists.

What was the pull to this remote, exotic place? It was off the beaten trail! But more so, it was its uniqueness. It is a group of Hindu and Jain temples spread over a vast area. The temples have a rich display of intricately carved statues. They're famous for their erotic sculptures, scenes of everyday life and various aspects of Hinduism.

The detail that went into the carvings on each temple was incredible. Both the outside and inside of the temples had carvings. It was mindboggling to imagine that someone spent years creating these masterpieces.

One of our guest house was in a field near the entrance to the site. We were in an oasis of nature and beauty. No motorized vehicles were here other than the daily bus; there were very few people and we were surrounded by rich green fields bordered with trees. We spent our days wandering from temple to temple and soaking up the natural beauty around us. A much needed break from the bustling Indian cities.

As alluring as it was to rest here for a while, we eventually felt the pull to keep moving.

We went back to the train station, where we took an overnight train to Varanasi. Up to this point our train experiences in India had been pleasant, but that was about to change. From previous experience, we booked a second-class sleeper. We were surprised to see people sitting in the aisle, between the seats, lying in the luggage racks, and jammed in our reserved seats. Every inch of space was covered.

The conductor helped us claim our reserved seats, and we sat down with our backpacks on our laps. We had no other place to put them. When the railway staff pulled down the bunks for the night, we climbed into them, and lying down, we covered our packs with our bodies. Before long, people were sitting at the end of the bunk. Needless to say, we didn't get much sleep.

We arrived in Varanasi before sunrise. We planned to stay in the train station until daylight, but that idea vanished when we saw the sea of humanity sitting or lying on every available space. We exited the station to find a rickshaw driver willing to take us to a guest house.

As it was very early, the guest house was closed. We rang the doorbell and waited, prepared to sit outside until it opened. Much to our surprise, someone opened the door. When we explained our dilemma, they informed us that they wouldn't know if there was space available until after checkout, which was a few hours away. We were tired and desperate!

The owner generously invited us to come in and wait in the dining room. Within minutes, we spread out our *sarongs* on the floor and were fast asleep. We woke up to the sound of movement in the kitchen.

As we waited for someone to check out, we ate breakfast and talked with the other guests. As luck would have it, a room came available, and we could sleep for a few more hours.

Our time in Varanasi was overwhelming.

We don't remember events; what we remember is the feeling from the event. That was true of my experience in Varanasi. It took me out of my comfort zone. It was overwhelming. Even as I sit here now writing about the experience, I can still feel the tightness in my body.

Varanasi is considered the spiritual capital of India. Thousands of people arrive daily to bathe in the sacred Ganges River, to perform burial rites and as a key tourist destination.

Everywhere we went, we were shoulder-to-shoulder with others. We visited a few temples where monkeys roamed freely, grabbing whatever wasn't out of sight or tied down. This meant items like glasses, wallets, cameras, bags, or jewelry. They even reached into pockets. My glasses went into a zipped pocket of my bag, which I clung to with both arms. Being nearsighted meant everything was blurred. I didn't dare take out my camera. I found the experience very unpleasant!

At dawn, we joined others on the obligatory boat ride on the Ganges River. Where I saw bits of human remains floating in the water from the pyres that didn't burn well. We watched as people bathed and drank the polluted river water. It was an onslaught of the senses, with a kaleidoscope of people, textures, colours, and activities. The air was filled with the acrid smell of smoke mingled with burning flesh. People chanted mantras, bells tinkled, cows mooed, people shouted, and loved ones cried. All of this added to the cacophony of noise.

We lasted only a few days.

Our next destination was Calcutta, or Kolkata as it is called today, where we hoped to get travel passes for Sikkim in the Himalayas.

Like Varanasi, Calcutta was a crowded city; however, it wasn't as overwhelming as Varanasi. Calcutta's one aspect that was difficult for me to accept was the vast numbers of people begging on the streets, many of them with physical impairments. If you gave something to the one person, several others would mob you. It was heart-wrenching.

We stayed at a guest house a few blocks away from Mother Teresa's orphanage, and one day we spent a few hours playing with the kids. It was a delight! The other days were spent in government offices where we attempted to get a travel permit for Sikkim, without any success. This changed our travel plans.

As we considered the time left on our tourist visa, we decided to head across the country to Bombay, today called Mumbai, then wind our way south. This time, we didn't hesitate. It was a first-class private compartment all the way.

A few days later, we were in Bombay. We found a lovely guest house a few blocks from the famous Gateway of India. The guest house was also close to the famous Taj Mahal Palace, the hotel where we splurged on lunch and drinks one day.

During our time in Bombay, we collected our mail at the American Express Office, wrote our letters, extended our tourist visa, planned our next destination, and wandered our way around the city. We were tired from three months of hardcore travelling.

In the end, we ended up in Goa. In the '80s, Goa was a free-spirit destination with nude beaches, cheap accommodation, beach parties, and a laid back atmosphere. Are you wondering if I went nude? No, only topless!

We rented a one-room mud hut from a wonderful family. Two other couples were staying there. It was like living in a large extended family. Our host family enfolded us into the family. We ate with them, celebrated Christmas with them, and shared yard work with them. It was our home away from home.

It didn't take us long to settle in. We rented bikes and soon had a daily routine. We woke up with the rooster, who crowed under our open window each morning. We did our morning ablutions at an outdoor sink, then hopped on our bikes and rode to our favourite beach restaurant for breakfast. After breakfast, we parked ourselves on the beach where we read, swam, and talked to others until early afternoon. On our way out, we stopped for lunch at the restaurant and rode back to our hut. We hand washed our clothes, had a siesta, and sat in the garden with our friends. It was a well-deserved rest.

The only real excitement we had happened on New Year's Eve when a colony of army ants came crawling in through the paneless window, over part of the bed, across the floor, over our friend's backpack, and out the other window. This colony was about a foot-and-a-half wide with no end in sight.

There wasn't much we could do in this situation, except get out of the way. It was a good thing we were off to a New Year's Eve party on the beach. By the time we came home at dawn, they'd moved on.

After a month of beach life, we were rested and ready to continue travelling.

# Chapter Twenty
## Opium Fields, Guns, and a Night of Tension

In late January of 1986, Karen and I landed in Bangkok, Thailand. It was like a breath of fresh air. After seven months of being on the road exploring Africa and India, travelling in Thailand was a breeze.

It didn't take long for us to get settled on Khao San Road, the traveller's oasis in the heart of Bangkok. In the '80s, it was one street lined with guest houses and restaurants. This was the place to meet other travellers, to get the scoop on the dos and don'ts of travelling in Thailand, and to enjoy fabulous Thai food. We spent a couple of weeks exploring Bangkok on foot, by *tuk-tuk* (the three-wheeled motorcycle taxis that precariously wove in and out of traffic), and in crowded city buses. Then, it was time to venture out and see more of the country.

We boarded a train and headed north to Chiang Mai. The sleeper trains in Thailand were an absolute luxury. They had privacy curtains, food and drink service, clean and spacious compartments, and friendly staff.

By now, I'd become a bit of an expert on train travel. Not surprising for the daughter of a railway employee who grew up surrounded by trains.

Chiang Mai in 1986 was a joy. It's the northern capital of Thailand, nestled in the land of misty mountains with its many colourful hill tribes, today called Highland Thais. It was the lure of trekking to these remote hill tribe villages that enticed us to the area.

It was simple to make arrangements to go trekking in the mountains. The travel agents came to us at the guest house. Even in the '80s, Thailand was geared up for tourists, especially backpackers.

Once we made our plans, we each packed a small day pack, placed our large backpacks in storage, and locked our valuables in the safe. We were travelling light with only the essentials: some clothes, a *sarong*, extra flip flops, some cash, and our passports. Everything else was locked up at the guest house. We were eager for this new adventure.

At daybreak, we boarded a minivan that would take us to Chiang Rai. At the time of our visit, it was also the illegal hub for the opium trade. It was from here that we started the trek into the mountains (from a Canadian perspective, foothills).

Although we were in the mountains, we were still in the tropics and the midday heat could reach 30 to 35C degrees. To make the most of the cool mornings, we were up and walking shortly after sunrise. The first day of our trek took us through lush green rice fields, which eventually brought us to the base of the hills. As we slowly climbed the hills, we came upon the infamous poppy fields. In the fields, men and women were meticulously making a slight slash on the poppy bulb from which a black substance oozed out; this was the opium. I was curious about what they were doing and they were willing to show me. How else does one learn about things, if one doesn't show interest?

Around mid-afternoon, we arrived tired and sweaty at the first village. This was a village of the Akha people. Our guide had divided the hiking group into twos and threes and allocated us to a host family. Our respective host families welcomed us with friendly, big smiles, and showed us to our sleeping area.

Almost all the houses in the various villages we visited were built on stilts for several reasons. This construction kept homes cooler by allowing the air to flow through, prevented flooding during monsoons, and provided a shady area for both people and animals.

Invariably, it was always the children who were the most eager to engage with us. It didn't take very long for a soccer game to start or for a group of children to gather around. They also loved to have their picture taken.

In each village, we shared a meal with our host family. The menu was pretty much the same in each village: fried rice with vegetables and mystery meat. Before leaving Chiang Mai, other travellers warned us that we might be eating dog meat. To be honest with you, by the time that the evening meal arrived I was so hungry that I didn't care what I was eating. The food was delicious. That was good enough for me.

Each morning, our host families served us a bowl of rice soup, which is a common breakfast in Thailand. The host families also packed us lunch: stirfry rice and vegetables, with or without meat, and sometimes a boiled egg, all secured in a plastic bag.

We stayed one night in a Karen village and another in a Lisu village. On the fourth day, we headed to a Lahu village; this was our last night in the hills before we returned to Chiang Rai. This particular day of trekking was rather difficult with a lot of steep inclines and descents. In addition to that, it was a hot, humid day. By the time we reached the Lahu village, we were xhausted.

We marched into the village anticipating a warm welcome, a beverage nd a meal, and a place to rest our weary bones.

Instead, we entered what looked like a deserted village. Our guide slowly aised his hand, indicating for us to slow down. As we slowed our pace, omeone began shouting at us. Our guide whispered for us to stop and not nove. He informed us that there were several guns pointed at us. We stood ooted to the spot, barely breathing. There was a brief exchange between ur guide and whoever was shouting. At the end of this exchange, our uide told us to slowly turn around and follow him out of the village.

As one, we turned and silently followed him to a spot some distance rom the village. He told us to sit down as he began to rummage through he foliage on the side of the path. He let out a stream of some choice Thai vords. He was obviously furious and upset.

He emerged from the bush holding a woven grass symbol. The village ad placed this sign on the path at the edge of the village so that no one vould enter the village.

Unfortunately, the sign had toppled over into the grass and out of sight. f our guide had seen the sign, we wouldn't have entered.

Now we were in trouble.

Many of the hill tribes have a strong belief in the spirit world. This articular village had just performed a special cleansing ceremony during vhich no outsiders were to enter the village. By entering the village, we'd efiled the ceremony. The villagers would now have to perform another eremony, which required more money. I don't think I have to tell you who vould be responsible for paying for it.

As we sat silently on grass along the path, our guide kept repeating over nd over again, "I am sorry. I am sorry. I am sorry." But it wasn't his fault!

Eventually, someone from the village came and guided us to a ilapidated tea shed on the periphery of the village. This was where we ere going to spend the night while our guide negotiated with the village lders on a fair price to redo the cleansing.

In the meantime, the women from the village sent us water, food, pium, and a potent home brew. We spread out our *sarongs* on the vooden floor and settled in for the night. None of us were sure what the utcome would be, but we had to trust that our guide would get us out of the situation safely.

After eating, several members of our group participated in smoking opium while others sampled the liquor. I had a small drink of the liquor, but I wasn't interested in partaking in the opium. Perhaps under different circumstances I may have tried it, but as it was, I wanted to keep my wits about me. In all honesty, just breathing in the secondhand smoke from the pipes left me lightheaded and a bit nauseous.

Needless to say, it was a very long night. As I drifted in and out of sleep, I could hear the village chief and our guide conversing.

In the morning, our guide asked us to bring out all the money we had with us. We eagerly shared what we had. He carefully counted it out as we held our breath. He smiled and said this would be enough. We all let out a sigh of relief.

It didn't take us long to pack up and hit the trail.

As this was our last day, most of the way back was downhill. As we barreled down the hills, we laughed and cracked jokes, releasing our stress and tension.

There's nothing like a challenging situation to bond a group together. When we returned to Chiang Mai, we met for dinner and drinks before heading off in different directions.

One thing that I've gained from this and a few other incidents is that you never truly know how you'll behave or act in any circumstance until you're actually in that circumstance. Until you experience a situation for yourself, you have no idea what you'll do.

As a result, I find it hard to judge someone for their behaviour in extreme situations, knowing that I could act the same way or in a completely different way. I don't know what I would do, so how can I judge someone else?

You never know what's going to happen next.

# Chapter Twenty-One
# Running Out of Money: Stay or Leave?

After our exciting adventure in northern Thailand, Karen and I were back in tourist mode, making our way back to Bangkok.

Travelling slowly by bus, we travelled south, exploring the three Thai Kingdoms' sites: Sukhothai, Ayutthaya, and Bangkok. Each kingdom has its own unique architecture and style; both Sukhothai and Ayutthaya are UNESCO World Heritage Sites. Exploring the ruins and temples gave me a sense of Thailand's long and rich history.

One piece of information that makes Thailand unique is that it was never colonized. Europeans had colonized all the surrounding countries, but not Thailand.

Burma, known now as Myanmar, was one of the colonized countries that intrigued me. Any guesses as to where we went next?

Karen and I headed to the airport with a one-week tourist visa stamped in our passports and airplane tickets in our hands. We also carried with us a valuable piece of advice from our fellow travellers. This advice was rather risky, but it could prove to be beneficial if we chose to act on it. For several days, we pondered the pros and cons of the advice. In the end, we decided to take a chance and go for it.

Once we checked in at the airport, we made our way to the duty-free shop where each of us purchased a carton of Marlboro cigarettes and a bottle of whiskey. Other travellers who'd travelled to Burma told us that it would be easy to sell cigarettes and whiskey for local currency. This would help us pay for our travels in the country without eating into our foreign currency.

We reasoned that if we didn't sell the goods, Karen, a smoker, would have two cartons of cigarettes, and we'd both drink the whiskey.

As it turned out, our taxi driver was grateful to make the exchange with us. We tucked the goods under the taxi seat, and our driver slipped us an envelope with cash. It was enough money to pay for part of our stay in Burma.

With only a one-week visa, we had to be strategic about what we wanted to see and do. It wasn't an easy decision because I wanted to see all of it.

In the end, we decided to go to Bagan with its 2,000 pagodas, stupas, and temples. To get there, we travelled by train. It was an overnight journey in a train leftover from the British colonial period. The train cars were made of wood as were the seats. There were no sleeper cars. Most of us slept on *sarongs* on the wooden floor. Early in the morning, we arrived in the middle of nowhere to find pickup trucks waiting to take us to Bagan. Our group clambered into the back of the trucks, packed in like sardines, and headed down a dusty dirt road. We arrived in Bagan hot, sweaty, and caked in dust. Those of us who made the journey together instantly became friends.

In 1986, Bagan had only a few guest houses and a couple of restaurant. The pull was the site itself. The entire site is huge, but the main archaeological site is 13 km x 8 km. For several days, we explored the many temples, stupas, and pagodas on foot before we returned to Yangon.

Even though our time was short, this is one place I'm delighted to have seen long before it became popular and easy to access. There was something mystical about the place. As I sat high on a temple to watch the sunrise, I felt my spirit soar and forge a connection to that inner oneness.

Back in Thailand, we headed south to Koh Samui for some beach time before crossing the border into Malaysia and down to Singapore. We travelled south along the west side of Malaysia and returned to Thailand, travelling on Malaysia's east side. It was interesting to notice how each of the countries in southeast Asia were different in feel and culture. Much of it had to do with its history and colonial influence.

By now, we'd been on the road for almost a year, and Karen had to return to Canada as her sabbatical was coming to an end. I wasn't ready to leave, even though I was slowly running out of funds. That inner confidence that I'd easily find work, which was sparked in Kenya, still held strong. I knew I would be OK.

As Karen and I walked along Si Lom Road after dinner on our last night in Bangkok together, I looked up and saw a sign that said, "English teacher needed." We stopped, and I went in to investigate. I talked to the manager, who hired me on the spot as I had teaching credentials. He wanted me to start the next morning. However, I planned to go to the airport with Karen the next day, so I agreed to start the following day.

This was another case of things happening that I couldn't have imagined. This wasn't me creating anything or doing anything other than trusting that things would work out.

So began my nine-month stint as an illegal ESL language teacher. I say illegal, but even though foreign teachers didn't have a work permit, we paid taxes every month. Hundreds of native English speakers worked in a variety of language schools in Bangkok.

Even though I was working, I still had a visitor's visa, which meant that I was required to leave the country and renew my visa every three months. This entailed taking the overnight train to southern Thailand, crossing the border into Malaysia, and making my way to Penang to the Thai Consulate.

Many of us made this visa run so regularly that a couple of hostels had set themselves up as a go-between for those of us needing a visa and the visa office. For a small fee and, of course, room rental, hostel staff provided us with the paperwork to fill out and then took our passports and money for the visa to the visa office to be processed. The hostel staff returned our passports with the visa stamp two days later, and we went back to Bangkok.

There was a lot of trust involved. The first time I used this system, I didn't relax until I had my passport back in my hands. The second time I was welcomed back like family, and every time after that, it was just a relaxing few days in Penang.

My teaching opportunities also began to flourish. The first school paid me a low hourly wage, but it met my needs. Then one student recommended me to a business owner, who hired me to teach English to his staff in the evenings. I did this for a month, and then I came across a language school near the guest house where I lived. This school had a much wider reach and, of course, paid better. Because I was the only qualified teacher in the school, I was teaching classes to some of their largest clients, like the Thai Electrical Board executives. These assignments came with a huge pay increase. I worked at this school for nine months, and when I left Thailand, I had US$5,000. Not bad for someone who, 10 months earlier, had only $200 in her pocket.

As my bank account started to grow, I began to consider leaving Thailand, but where would I go? I was getting the urge to find a regular teaching job, and I wasn't ready to return to Canada. My problem was I had no idea how to find a school. I don't know why I didn't look for a school in Bangkok at that time, but I didn't. That would have to wait for several more years.

As I let the thought of finding a school rest within me, I felt drawn to the British Council, a British organization specializing in international cultural and educational opportunities. As I scanned the newspapers, I saw a few job ads; however, what caught my eye was ad for an International School Job Fair in London, England in February. The deadline for registering was coming up, and I'd have to act quickly. With help from the British Council staff, I completed the forms and sent them off before the deadline.

I was accepted, and thus began the next chapter for my life within the realm of international schools.

# Part Three: Climbing the International School Ladder

For most of us our cultural conditioning runs very deep. I'm no exception. At the deepest core level, I'm a free spirit, but at that time, my human self was still deeply tied to the conditioning of my upbringing. Somewhere in my human consciousness was the recording that played the tune, "It's time to get a real job. You can't keep wandering around the world. It's time to act like an adult." With my discovery of the International School system, I was able to meet the needs of my spirit as well as satisfy my cultural conditioning. Thus began my journey up the career ladder.

# Chapter Twenty-Two
## Freedom Fighters, Inflation, and Black Market Ventures

Once again, I was venturing into uncharted territory. Navigating the international school job fair was like walking in the dark without a light. I had to trust my instincts and ask for help when I drew a blank about what to do. At this point in my career, I didn't know what questions to ask about the schools or the countries where I'd potentially be teaching. I did know what I could do and that I was open to possibilities.

One never truly knows what one is getting into until one is in it.

That was true of my arrival in Lusaka, Zambia, in the late '80s. Of course, the school didn't tell their foreign teachers that Zambia was a home for freedom fighters from Zimbabwe, South Africa, Namibia, and Mozambique. Nor did they mention that the sanctions imposed on Zambia due to sheltering these individuals meant shortages of items such as food supplies, car parts, medicines, and toiletries. They also glossed over the fact that Zambia parted ways with the IMF (International Monetary Fund), which resulted in runaway inflation.

As a newbie in the country, none of this fully registered in my awareness until I began to witness the shrinking spending power of my incountry salary. I was now beginning to understand why the school paid most of our salary into bank accounts outside the country and the remainder in Kwacha (Zambian currency). Each month, the other teachers and I watched with horror as the inflation rate kept escalating at an alarming rate.

There was no way to bring money into the country, for no bank recognized Kwacha, and no bank would send money into the country. So, there I was with money in my external bank account and an ever-decreasing pool of money where I needed it most.

The situation was becoming very stressful, and I wasn't sure how I'd survive on a disappearing salary. I did consider breaking my contract, but I felt that something would show up. It always did. I sent my plea to the universe for a way to earn more money and then carried on.

The universe answered!

One day Monique, my housemate from France, introduced me to her friends at the French Embassy. Monique had mentioned to them that I spoke French and was an English teacher. It just so happened that they were looking for an English teacher for their embassy staff.

After three months in the country, I was teaching English at the French embassy two days a week for double the money I was making teaching full time at the International School. Voila, a new source of income had arrived.

Being the social butterfly that I was in those days, I soon made friends with the local community members. I had friends in the African, Indian, and expat communities.

Within the community, the main focus of everyone's attention was the sharply rising inflation rate. Many African and Indian businesspeople in Zambia had a lot of Kwacha but no way of getting hard currency (stable currency that won't depreciate or fluctuate in value). Without hard currency, they couldn't purchase materials, replacement parts, or anything else needed to keep their businesses running.

This opened up another revenue source for me. One of my business friends approached me with a business proposition that surprised me and caused me to evaluate the risk involved.

All foreign teachers at the school used the black market to exchange their stash of US dollars for Kwacha. I did, too! This was how many of us kept pace with inflation.

I went to my business friend when I needed a bit more local currency. He was happy to help me, as it provided him with a small amount of US dollars. In fact, it was with him that I exchanged money for a few other teachers and friends. So, it shouldn't have been a surprise when he suggested that I be his go-between with the school's teachers and some of my other friends in the money trading game. For each transaction, I would get a percentage of the exchange.

Thus began my short career as a black market trader.

A third, smaller money funnel came with forays into a local residential area for bread.

There were countrywide shortages of flour, sugar, salt, and cooking oil, which meant no bread or baking of any kind. Basically, if it wasn't grown in Zambia, it wasn't available. Luckily, Zambia's rich land produced an abundance of fruit, vegetables, and meat.

Smuggling became a way of life for many people, and almost everyone was in on it. A couple of my Zambian friends would bring in bread from

Zimbabwe and sell it on the black market. They'd let me know when the bread arrived. We'd arrange to meet in a local outdoor *shebeen* (bar) for a beer. While we sat under a tree chatting and sharing a beer, a third person would fill the trunk of my car with bread. After an hour or so, money casually exchanged hands, and I'd drive back to school with bread, which the staff gladly purchased.

There were risks involved, such as a jail term or deportation. I knew only too well the risks I was taking. Still, I never felt afraid. Given who I was then and the circumstances I was living in, I did what I thought was best at the time. I was surviving by accepting the opportunities that came my way.

I'm grateful to my friends in Zambia for providing me with a way to supplement my income by helping others.

Would I do it again? Possibly! In each moment and circumstance in life, we can only respond to what is presented to us at the moment.

Those years in Zambia showed me the resilience that I never knew I had.

Even though Zambia's economic situation was dire, the community spirit was strong, vibrant, and alive.

# Chapter Twenty-Three
## Adventures in Zambia

Inoticed over the years that when external circumstances are challenging, people rally together. There's a strong community spirit. That's what I found in Lusaka.

I lived in a townhouse in a compound that housed eight units. In the compound's centre was a swimming pool and a lovely brick barbecue, along with fruit trees around the periphery. Depending on the season, we had fresh mangos, guavas, papayas, avocados, and bananas. All of us teachers would come home from school to find a pile of fruit outside our door. As wonderful as this might sound, by the end of the season we were ready for the tree to stop producing. Imagine eating five or six large avocados every day for four months.

The barbecue and pool were the gathering point for many communal meals. Someone would light the barbecue, while the rest of us would dig out some meat, take stock of our veggies, and rummage through our pantries. Because of the shortages, sharing was a way of life. If one of us found something in the market, we bought enough for everyone or as much as we could. There was no hoarding or stashing away of goods. If you needed something, you checked with the others. If they had what you needed, they shared.

Our school, the International School of Lusaka (ISL), was another gathering point. It was a private school whose students came from the families at the embassies and other agencies. We had students from every corner of the world. By proxy, school staff was enfolded into the various communities within Lusaka. We were invited to all major and minor social events. I attended more formal balls in Lusaka than anywhere else I lived. There seemed to be a never-ending round of events, parties, and dinners to attend. At these social gatherings, I got to meet and party with several future heads of state.

In 1987, there was far less security than there is now. We popped in at the American Embassy to watch movies at the Marine House. I often drove to the Canadian Ambassador's house for afternoon tea or dropped things off without any security checks. I had friends in most embassies. It was normal to pile into vehicles with embassy plates and head off for the weekend. It was a very different world.

At ISL, I was introduced to the British curriculum. I fell in love with it, as I felt it was much more practical than the curriculum I'd been taught in Canada. I had a taste of it in Nigeria, but now I was immersed in it. It would come in handy down the road.

Besides the social scene, I had the opportunity to try a few new things, like tennis. Someone gifted me a membership to the Zambian Airways Tennis Club (ZATC) and I had weekly lessons from Zambian's second seed male tennis player. Most other expats belonged to the Lusaka Club; thus, I was the only White female member at ZATC. I didn't mind one bit, as I had a great tennis instructor and many friends in the club. In case you're wondering: no, my instructor wasn't the one who gifted me the membership. That will remain a secret.

My club friendships were a blessing when navigating Zambia's bureaucratic organizations.

One night after several days of heavy rain, a large branch from a huge rubber tree in our townhouse parking lot broke off, landed down in the middle of my car, and turned it into a V-frame. I needed a police report to claim insurance. Who better to write the report than the chief of police? He not only wrote the report, he also took me to the insurance office and introduced me to the lady in charge of my file. He told me to make sure I came back every week to personally move my file from section to section, or really from desk to desk. To reinforce the point, he led me to a room and opened the door. The room was full of files. I mean floor-to-ceiling and wall-to-wall. He informed me that this would be where my file would end up if I didn't come and move my file. I followed his instructions, and a month later, I received an insurance cheque. Receiving payment in such a short time was a very rare event. I have my Zambian friends to thank.

Something else I learned in Lusaka was scuba diving. Yup, Zambia is a landlocked country. But, Lusaka had a scuba diving club run by an ex-British Navy SEAL. The training took place in the local swimming pool beside the school. Nothing was unusual about that. However, to complete the qualification, one needed to do a couple of open water dives and a night dive at Lake Kariba.

Lake Kariba was formed when the Kariba Dam was built on the Zambezi River between 1958 and 1963. It's also home to Nile crocodiles and hippopotami.

OK, you can breathe now!

Yes, this was where I went for my qualifying dives.

The absurdity of the situation only hit when the scuba instructor handed high-calibre rifles to two of our team members, who would stay on the boat and be on the lookout for crocs and hippos. They assured us that it was rare for either of those visitors to show up in the deeper water.

My first daylight dive was fraught with more than a little fear. I made it a point to stay close to my instructor while constantly scanning the surrounding area. As I clambered into the boat at the end of the dive, it was with a sense of relief. On the subsequent dives, I was more relaxed. In fact, I ended up enjoying my time underwater.

In all, I completed four dives and earned my qualifications. I have to admit that diving in Lake Kariba was very boring. There was little to see except for some dead tree stumps, a few tigerfish, and lots of *kapenta*, a small sardine-like fish.

Now I was ready for real open water. A couple of months later I was on the island of Mauritius, diving in the Indian Ocean to see sunken ships and to swim along coral reefs. Now, that was diving.

Our most common weekend getaway was to Victoria Falls or *Mosi-oa-Tunya*, meaning "The Smoke that Thunders." My companions and I drove down on a Friday afternoon and easily returned on a Sunday. Victoria Falls had only one major hotel with decent rooms, a good bar (subject to liquor shortages), an OK restaurant, and a fresh water swimming pool. I loved sitting beside the falls and listening to the thundering water. We sat on the rocks at the edge of the falls and looked down during the dry season. I feel so grateful for the many visits to the falls; I experienced its personality in all seasons.

The frequent trips to the falls were for more than pleasure. It always included a walk across the bridge into Zimbabwe to go shopping for those essential items we couldn't find in Zambia. You know, like toothpaste, soap, shampoo, sugar, coffee, cheese, and more. We were limited to what we could carry back. It was best to go as a group and combine our lists. Then we could combine items, buying only one large package of something and dividing it later. We became experts at maximizing our shopping expeditions, purchasing enough goods to last a month or more. Also, we only bought what we needed. There were no luxury items, well... maybe chocolate!

On occasion, several of us ventured out on safari in Zambia, Zimbabwe, and Botswana. Zambia had few tourists in those days, which kept the cost low, and there were always vacancies in the lodges.

One of our favourite safari spots was in the Kafue National Park in northern Zambia, where we stayed in a beautiful lodge in a serene setting.

At that time, Zambia was one of the few countries that offered walking safaris. As a kid growing up, I loved trekking in the bush with my dad, so this walking safari was right up my alley.

I was up at the crack of dawn, ready to go. As we walked away from the lodge into the bush, there were four of us with a guide who carried a hunting rifle. I knew how to walk without making a sound. As I put each foot down, the rest of my senses were on high alert, just as my father taught me. We slowly made our way through the trees, and then our guide stopped and indicated with his hand for us to stop. What did he see? I followed his gaze, and there she sat: a lioness watching a herd of gazelle.

As I stood watching this beautiful lioness several metres in front of me, it took everything I had not to walk up and pet her. We watched her for a while as she twitched her tail and eyeballed her next meal.

After a while, we slowly moved downwind to check out a herd of zebras and wildebeests. These two animals always travel together since wildebeests have better hearing, while zebras have better sight. It's always great to have an ally that can warn you in case of any impending danger.

We started to make our way back to the lodge when we came across a small gang of Cape Buffalo. We gave this herd a wide berth, for these animals can be very dangerous if they're bothered.

Walking in the bush and getting a close up view of the animals that lived there was the perfect way for me to start my day.

Later that day, we piled onto benches in the back of a pickup truck and headed out for the evening safari. While we drove around in search of the game, I felt something bite my thigh. I was so engrossed in looking for wildlife that I ignored the bite. Only when my leg began to seriously swell did I give it notice. I called out to our guide, who stopped the truck and looked at the bite. He then informed me it was from a tsetse fly and told the driver to return to the lodge.

I knew I was having an allergic reaction because I had a severe allergy to fish at that time. I also knew there were antihistamines in my luggage at the lodge, and this was a blessing because the nearest hospital was a plane ride away, and the plane wasn't due till morning. Back at the lodge, I took two antihistamines, ate dinner, fell asleep, and woke up the next morning with the swelling gone and ready for another adventure.

As I mentioned earlier, I don't give energy to the "what could've happened" scenarios. When the event is over, and I've done all that I can do to deal with it, I let it go and move on.

The tsetse fly was one thing; having to deal with a pod of hippopotami was another thing. This encounter took place in Chobe National Park in Botswana.

After a full day of game viewing in the park, I took a shower, changed my clothes, and ate a gourmet meal of ostrich steak. Then, my two friends and I retired to the lounge for a nightcap. As usual, we began chatting with the other guests, comparing our lists of animal sightings.

During our conversation, we noticed the staff bringing in foam mattresses, blankets, and pillows. They also closed the patio doors to the veranda. Someone mentioned that perhaps it was closing time, and we should head back to our chalets. Just then, the staff informed us that we'd be spending the night on the floor in the lounge because the hippos were onshore and had cut off the path to the chalets.

Hippos are water creatures. They feel safe there. At night they come out of the water to graze the grass along the river's edge. When away from the water, they spook easily and will head back to the river, attacking anything in their path. Thus, it was unsafe for us to go back to the chalets. There was nothing for us to do except claim a mattress, curl up, and go to sleep. One doesn't negotiate with a 1,500 kg frightened hippo.

Throughout all of these experiences, Zambia showed me the importance of community. It's there I learned to share, to be resourceful, to be frugal, and to accept opportunities that I might otherwise pass up.

Some might call this time a hardship, but I see it as an amazing experience in navigating the waters of life. Each of us is so much more capable than we think we are.

When my contract came up for renewal at the end of the second year, and the economic situation in Zambia appeared to be getting worse rather than better, I decided it was time to try another school.

# Chapter Twenty-Four
## Life Can Change in an Instant

In February of 1989, I was off to my second job fair. This time, I had a better idea of what to expect and how to prepare for the interviews. I was still a newbie and green, but I was confident and excited to find out where I'd be going.

Like any other job fair, there's no certainty that you'll come away with a job, and in an international job fair setting, there's no saying where you might end up. It all depended on which school needed your specialization, and if the school resonated with you.

In many ways, this suited my personality. I've always been comfortable with not knowing and with being open to new adventures. The one thing that I had going for me was that I was qualified to teach both history and English.

I loved being back in London, England, where I was able to connect with friends as well as take in a play or two in the West End. And, do a little shopping on Oxford Street.

When I picked up my information package on the first day of the job fair, I was surprised to see that I'd been invited to interview with three different Kuwait school representatives. Not one, but three!

Perhaps I wasn't totally surprised, because for a year I listened as my colleague, who'd lived in Kuwait, regaled us with stories of her life there. I must admit I was intrigued. Her experiences in Kuwait shattered many of my preconceived ideas of the Middle East. As a result, I curiously went to the interviews.

You guessed right! I accepted a job at Al Bayan Bilingual School (BBS). I managed to convince the school director that I could teach IB (International Baccalaureate) history, even though I had no idea what IB was or what the curriculum looked like. Later as I dove into the program, I discovered it was an academically challenging European program for grade 11 and 12 students. As I reflect on that interview, I'm amazed at my confidence and ability to persuade someone to hire me.

Once again, I found myself immersed in a completely new culture. As I navigated my way through a modern airport, I was all eyes and ears. I tuned into the melody of Arabic as my eyes took in men dressed in *thobes* and women dressed in *abayas, hijabs,* and chic Western outfits. It was all so new and exciting!

It didn't take me long to adjust! After several years of living on a shoestring budget, I felt like I'd won the lottery. I was in a country where I could buy anything and everything. I was earning a great salary, I was working with wonderful colleagues who quickly became friends, and I was enjoying a challenging job. In addition to this, I had a side gig tutoring the children of a wonderful Kuwaiti family.

My time in Egypt prepared me for what to wear and how to behave in a Muslim country. I enjoyed going out to a variety of restaurants, sitting under palm trees, sharing a *shisha* pipe with friends, attending camel races, going on boating adventures, enjoying picnics in the desert, sleeping under the stars, and attending parties and special events with both my new Arabic and expat friends. Life was great!

One friend I'm grateful to have had was Adul Ghani, the Islamic teacher in our school. Adul Ghani was a quiet, gentle, patient man who always had time to answer my many questions about Islamic and Arabic culture. We all called him by his full name as a sign of respect. He often invited me to his home for a meal and to spend time with his family. He helped me to open my eyes to the beauty of the culture that I was immersed in. The wisdom he shared with me gave a new perspective with which to view the Arabic world. It's been a great gift!

For the first time in many years, I had a consistently growing bank account, and I was confident that it would continue to grow. I was prepared to stay in Kuwait teaching at BBS for many years. With this mindset, I planned a summer adventure in Europe with Athens as my base.

When I was in Athens, I stayed with Christine, who I'd met in Bangkok. I was happy to be back in Athens after so many years. The flame in my heart that was lit in 1979 during my first trip to Greece was stirred again as I wandered the Acropolis, the Parthenon, and the Plaka. This time I also got to know what it was like to live in Athens as Christine and I did the shopping or took her twin boys on walks or to the park.

From Athens I flew to Finland, where I joined a Smithsonian tour. I'm not usually one to go on a tour, but this one appealed to me because of the route it took.

The tour travelled by bus through northern Finland from Helsinki, spending some time in Lapland with the reindeer farmers. Our next destination was Kirkenes, Norway, a small town above the Arctic circle. In the summertime at this latitude, the sun never sets. Several of us stayed up all night and marveled at how the sun sat just above the western horizon at sunset, and then throughout the night moved across the sky to the east where it began a new day.

Very early in the morning, our group boarded a bus and made our way to the then-Soviet border of Borisoglebsk. During the Cold War, this was a very sensitive border crossing. We were the first tour group to be allowed to cross the border at this point since it was closed at the beginning of the Communist period. When we were on the Soviet side of the border, we were taken by bus to Nikel to catch the train going south into Russia.

In Russia, we visited Murmansk, Petrozavodsk, Leningrad, and on to Moscow. We also visited Riga in Latvia. This trip was notable in two ways. First, this was my second trip to Russia. The first time I went to Russia was in 1981 during the Communist period, when a fellow teacher and myself took high school students to Russia. Now here I was in 1989, returning to Russia during the *glasnost* ("openness" in Russian) period, which was the loosening of the Communist grip. This historical time frame wasn't lost on me.

Besides exploring the usual tourist sites, I got to board a huge icebreaker (a ship that moves through icy waters) in Murmansk. In Petrozavodsk, I attended an evening street dance with live music that lasted till dawn. On the island of Kizhi, we visited a beautiful wooden church that miraculously wasn't destroyed during the Communist period, and we were entertained by older women singing and dancing with pure joy.

While we were in Leningrad, we could wander around the city, something I couldn't do in 1981. Ellie, a member of the tour, and I went out looking for a synagogue she knew about. Our taxi driver spoke English and acted as our tour guide. This little side trip took us into a residential part of Leningrad most tourists don't see and a resident rabbi gave us a rare tour of the synagogue.

We were also able to wander on our own around Nevsky Prospekt, the shopping area, and were able to venture out for dinner at a local restaurant. Having experienced the restrictions of my previous visit, this freedom added to the richness of my trip.

Our arrival in Riga, Latvia, coincided with their annual music festival. There were street performances in the city centre and an open-air concert in the evening. It was one of the most beautiful concerts I've ever attended. Even though I didn't understand the words, I felt the emotion and passion n the songs and witnessed the tears of those listening. It was a powerful performance by people who had suffered much under communism.

One evening in Moscow, I attended a local house party with the group's Smithsonian historian. Fred still had many friends in Moscow from his university days. We took the metro, with its stunning artwork and beauty, to a suburb with high-rise buildings. We entered a communal apartment building with a shared cooking area and bathroom but with a private sitting room and bedrooms. It was a memorable evening of eating, drinking, singing, and talking. I didn't understand Russian, but one lady spoke some Ukrainian, which I could follow. Fred was a great translator. To return to the city centre, we stood outside under a street light and waited for a taxi to show up. While we stood there, our hosts began to sing. It was truly a night to remember.

I returned to Athens tired and fulfilled. Christine's home was in Athens' centre, so I spent a few days visiting my favourite sites, doing my laundry, and playing with her twin boys. I love Greece and enjoyed my time there.

Before long, I was off on my next adventure. I flew to Paris to meet my friend Farah, who was joining me from Canada. This was my summer to explore Europe in a way I couldn't before.

Farah and I spent several days in Paris and the surrounding area before we headed to Spain. In Spain, we followed the tourist route: Madrid, Seville, Toledo, Granada, Córdoba. Of course, we didn't miss the beaches. Many different cultures influence Spain's rich history. As a result, each area of the country has a slightly different flavour. One place I enjoyed was Granada and the Alhambra complex with its gardens, mosque, and towers.

The other place I found fascinating was Córdoba with its blend of Moorish and Christian architecture. We also enjoyed the old town with its narrow streets and nooks and crannies all over the place.

During our travels in Spain, we became friends with Darcy and Maria, Brazilian couple who encouraged us to join them for 10 days in Morocco. It sounded like a great idea. Before we knew it, we were on a ferry crossing the Mediterranean into Africa. I have to admit that over the years, Africa has always pulled me like a giant magnet.

We had a blast in Morocco with Darcy and Maria. We had a tour guide for most of our adventures in Morocco, but we also had Farah, whose first language is Arabic, so we had an added advantage.

Morocco was a beautiful blending of African and Arabic cultures.

We landed in Tangier and headed directly to Fez. The streets are narrow, are for pedestrians only, and are a great place to stroll and absorb the atmosphere and shop.

We followed up with visits to Meknes, Marrakesh, Casablanca, and Rabat. Although each place was interesting, it's Fez that stands out in my mind. I loved its rich history and got a sense of a life so different from the modern world we live in.

It was time to head back north, as both Farah and I had planes to catch in Paris. Back in Tangier, we boarded the next ferry back to Spain. While we were on the ferry, Darcy and Maria came rushing over to us from the concession booth and asked me, "You work in Kuwait don't you?" I replied that I did. Darcy looked me in the eyes and said, "I don't think you do anymore." I asked, "Why not?" He replied, "Iraq has invaded Kuwait."

It took a moment for that information to sink in. I couldn't quite believe it. Somewhere within me, I thought this won't last long because Kuwait had always been able to deal with Iraq. I was wrong.

The date was Aug. 2, 1990, the day when my world got flipped upside down.

# Chapter Twenty-Five
# Grief Came in Waves

The ferry crossing from Morocco to Spain on Aug. 2, 1990, radically changed that memorable summer energy. My carefree attitude and confidence that I'd be returning to Kuwait and Al Bayan Bilingual School (BBS) were replaced with uncertainty and concern. Underlying the concern was a trust that everything would work out. Initially, I was quite confident that Iraq and Kuwait would work things out, but as the weeks went by, I realized that this wasn't going to happen. I needed another plan. But, what plan?

I said goodbye to Farah in Paris and made my way back to Athens, Greece. I wasn't sure what I was going to do. The best I came up with was a wait-and-see attitude.

I arrived in Athens thinking I'd stay with my friend Christine. As things turned out, a friend of hers was returning to England for a couple of months. Her friend was happy for me to stay temporarily in her apartment, which was a 15-minute walk from Christine's house and in the heart of Athens. You may call it luck, synchronicity, or destiny. I call it trust. Trust that everything was going to work out just fine.

Once I settled back in Athens, I called one of my sisters to let my family know that I was going to stay in Athens for the time being. During this call, my sister relayed a message from Diane, a BBS colleague. Diane urgently wanted me to call her. It had something to do with a job possibility.

The call to my sister set in motion a whole chain of amazing happenings. I called Diane, who informed me that the director of an international school in Malta was looking for a social studies/history teacher to start in September. I called the Verdala International School Malta and spoke to the director. He was impressed with my qualifications and experience and wanted to hire me. Before he could do that, he had to get permission from the Maltese government. The problem was that all of my professional papers were in Kuwait. I had no proof of anything except my citizenship with my passport.

Several phone calls later, I had another job. The Maltese government agreed to let me start teaching without my papers. While I waited for the school to sort out the travel details, I spoke with my sister, who agreed to contact the universities and Alberta Teachers' Association for duplicates of my certificates.

At the end of August 1990, I was on my way to Malta. I arrived with one suitcase and a carry-on bag that contained my summer travelling clothes and a couple of souvenirs. Everything else I had in the world was in Kuwait.

The school provided housing for teachers who accepted the role of boarding parents for the international students. I agreed to be a boarding parent and had a large, one-bedroom apartment in the boarding complex. Since I arrived with virtually nothing, the director and his wife helped me to get the basics for my new home.

At this point in my life, it didn't take me very long to settle in and adjust to a new country and school. I had fulfilling work, wonderful colleagues, and thoughtful care packages from my family and friends in Canada.

Once the school year began and I settled into a routine, I began to reflect on what was happening in Kuwait. I was in touch with several colleagues from Kuwait and was glued to the news.

Before I arrived in Malta, I'd already gone through grief's stages of shock and denial. That was mild compared to the stages of grief that were yet to come.

In my daily life, I was surrounded by people who felt that Kuwait was getting its just reward. I tried to tell them what I knew and experienced, but it fell on deaf ears. My perspective was different from theirs. My experiences in Kuwait had given me a completely different view of the situation. I was angry and hurt by their opinions. I had trouble understanding their point of view. I felt alone and isolated.

The more news I heard from friends and colleagues in Kuwait, the more I felt guilty because I was safe, I had work, and I wasn't living in fear. This guilt left me feeling helpless and even more isolated.

Several teachers from BBS were taken as hostages to Iraq, while other friends and their families fled Kuwait to Saudi Arabia or other countries on foot with little food or water. I heard of others who were tortured. This wasn't a war on the other side of the world. It was personal for me because of the bonds I'd made and the people I knew. I was torn with sadness and concern for those in Kuwait. I shed many tears for those who died, who were maimed, or who were affected by the war. My heart ached.

Then there was the grief from personal loss. I grieved for items that had sentimental significance. I grieved for things that I believed gave me security. I grieved for the loss of a way of life that I felt was mine. I grieved for what could've been.

The grief came in waves. Eventually, the peaks and troughs of grief gave way to gentler ripples. It was in the ripples that I began to glean the gems hidden in the debris. Each level of grief contained an element of release. It allowed me to let go and made it possible for my life to carry on.

I came away from this experience with several important perspectives. I realized that loss is a normal part of life, that everything can change in the blink of an eye, and that all material items can be replaced. Today, I have little attachment to things. I also realized that grief is a process that can't be hurried or dismissed; it needs to be felt and allowed to pass through. I also recognized the importance of forgiveness. Forgiveness is a powerful healing tool. Forgive others if they don't understand. Forgive yourself for the anger, guilt, or sadness that arises. Forgive those who perpetrate war and suffering. Most of all, be gentle with yourself, for this too shall pass.

Needless to say, this experience changed me on several layers. Life as I knew it wouldn't be the same.

# Chapter Twenty-Six
## Let Me Keep My Swimsuit

Although my year in Malta was clouded by the events taking place in the Middle East, I enjoyed the small school atmosphere, explored the diverse history of Malta, embarked on a side trip to Sicily, and developed friendships that are still strong today.

As the school year was drawing to a close, I felt the pull to move on. As I sit writing this, I have no recollection of what prompted me to leave. All I know is that life leads me in mysterious ways, and I always land exactly where I need to be.

I landed back in Africa! This time I went to Maseru, Lesotho, a tiny kingdom surrounded by South Africa.

In 1991, South Africa still had the policy of apartheid, and Lesotho was a haven for many freedom fighters. In fact, many of our students were children of wellknown ANC (African National Congress) leaders who went on to become world-famous. I had parent/teacher conferences with a few of them.

For many years, I avoided travelling to South Africa because of apartheid and because I didn't want a South African stamp in my passport. At that time, many countries, especially African countries, wouldn't allow you entry if you'd travelled there. This was especially true of many African countries.

This may not have been a problem, except for the fact that almost all of our shopping trips, medical and dental appointments, and holiday destinations were in South Africa. To get around this issue, the Canadian Embassy issued us a second passport exclusively for crossing the border from Lesotho into South Africa.

The move to Lesotho was the energy shift I needed in order to let go of the grief that pulled me down in Malta. I was in a larger school and once again teaching IB history. I didn't know it at the time, but the IB program would form the basis of the rest of my career. In addition, teaching at Machabeng International School gave me a solid footing in the world of international schools. It opened the door to the University of Bath and a master's degree in educational management.

Living in Lesotho, I had the Drakensberg Mountains as my playground.

I love mountains! I spent weekends with my colleagues trekking and camping in the mountains. Being immersed in nature was a balm for my soul. Africa healed me.

Outside of Lesotho was the whole of South Africa with its vineyards, beaches, plains, mountains, wildlife reserves and the diversity of its cities: Durban, Johannesburg, Bloemfontein, Pretoria, and Cape Town. I'm so happy that I got to travel so extensively through this beautiful land.

Just outside of South Africa was Namibia in the Kalahari Desert with some of the world's most spectacular sand dunes. There was also Swaziland (now called the Kingdom of Eswatini), Mozambique, and Botswana.

What can I say? I love Africa! She won my heart once again.

I probably would have stayed in Lesotho longer had it not been for one incident.

One beautiful, bright Sunday, a group of us teachers headed off to the swimming pool at the only major hotel in Maseru. After several hours of swimming and lounging around the pool with my friends, I decided I'd had enough and was ready to go home. I'd gotten there by car with my friends, but they weren't ready to leave. So, I decided I'd walk home. It wasn't that far and it was a nice day.

On my way home, I stopped to pick up something in a small convenience store. I made my purchase, left the store, and began to walk up the hill towards my house. The way home had two possible routes. The long way was to walk along the road through the residential area, and the short way was to take a well-used path that cut between two properties. I almost always used the shortcut and that day was no different.

About halfway up the hill, I felt the presence of someone behind me. I glanced back to see three young men following me. My internal antenna shot up, and I knew something wasn't quite right. As I walked, I ran through the options of staying on the road or taking the shortcut. I decided on the shortcut.

A few metres into the shortcut, two of the boys raced ahead of me. A short distance away from me, they stopped and stood as if they were going to urinate against the fence. This wasn't an unusual sight. I kept walking, although by now I knew that something was wrong.

As I approached the two boys, the third boy came up from behind, grabbed me from the back, and held a knife to my throat

At this point, everything became surreal. I don't think I've ever been as fully present as I was at that moment.

Strangely enough, I wasn't afraid. The first thought I recall having was that the knife at my throat was dull and it would hurt if it was used. I also knew that the boys only wanted my money. I was OK parting with my money, but I wanted to keep my bathing suit and day pack. Don't ask me why, for I've no idea what I was thinking at that moment.

When the boys demanded my money, I responded by saying, "I will give you my wallet with all my money, but please let me keep my day pack and swimsuit."

Immediately, I felt the arm holding me and the knife against my throat relax slightly. I also felt an energy shift; there was a dramatic pause as the boys processed my ridiculous request. In that space of their confusion, I held up my right hand and said, "I will put my hand in my bag and bring out my wallet. You can have it. Is that OK with you?" They replied, "Yes", and that's exactly what I did.

The second that I took the wallet out of my bag, one boy whipped it out of my hand, and they ran off. I was left with my day pack and my swimsuit.

As I started to walk the short distance to the road ahead, my body began to react and I started to tremble. Fortunately, the house directly across the street from the shortcut was the school director's. I knocked on the door and his wife greeted me, took one look at me, and dragged me inside. I stayed with them until my body and mind began to return to normal.

This was Africa in the '90s and there was no calling the police to report the crime. At that time, it was common to have to offer a bribe to the police and then have to negotiate with them. Besides, I only had a small amount of money in my wallet and I wasn't physically hurt.

Although I wasn't hurt, this incident did affect me for the rest of my stay in Lesotho. From that day on, I drove everywhere. I was always aware of who was behind me. And, my safety antenna was always alert when I was out and about.

Another thing that getting mugged revealed to me was that you never know what you're going to do or how you're going to react in any situation. You might play scenarios out in your mind, but this incident showed me that those scenarios we envision rarely happen as we think. Something deep within you will take over and you have no idea what it might be.

It also made me aware of how absolutely clear your thinking becomes when you're totally focused in the moment. All the distracted thinking stops when every part of you is tuned into that moment and you become so aware of everything that's going on. You're crystal clear.

A few months after this incident I started to get headaches, which for me is extremely rare. I went to my doctor in South Africa, who ran various tests and prescribed a few treatments, but the headaches persisted. He referred me to specialists who ran all sorts of tests on me, but they couldn't figure out what was wrong.

It wasn't until one afternoon as I was driving home from another round of medical appointments that I realized I was still holding onto the fear from the mugging. From that moment on, the headaches disappeared.

As much as I loved living in South Africa, I needed to leave Lesotho.

So, I began to prepare for another job fair in London. As I gathered the paperwork necessary to apply for the job fair, I realized I needed some documents from the school in Kuwait.

It was 1993, the war between Iraq and Kuwait had ended, and the school had partially opened. Deep within me, I was waiting for the middle school and high school to open up in the hope that I could return.

In the meantime, I had to get my documents from them. I picked up the phone and called the school in Kuwait. Much to my surprise, the receptionist who answered the phone was the same receptionist as before. After sharing the joy of reconnecting, she told me they were opening the schools in September and they were hiring. She asked me to hold the line, as she was sure the director would want to speak to me. Sure enough, Kadija, the director and a dear friend of mine, was overjoyed to find out I was looking for a job and hired me over the phone. I was on my way back to Kuwait.

Since I already had a flight booked to London for the job fair, I decided to take a short holiday. Off I went to London and returned to Lesotho to end the school year.

Even though I was excited to be returning to Kuwait, I was a little nervous of what I would find there after the Gulf War.

I had changed and Kuwait had changed. How would this play out?

# Chapter Twenty-Seven
## Off Balance

The previous four years had changed me. In many ways, it knocked me off balance. I welcomed some changes, but other changes left me feeling lost, and for the first time in my life, unsure of myself.

I had changed and Kuwait had changed. We were both finding our way in a new time and space.

I returned to Kuwait in mid-August 1993. I landed at Kuwait International Airport late in the evening. All flights arrived and departed at night because the daytime temperatures were too hot.

The airport hadn't changed much, and waiting for me were several familiar faces. It was a wonderful, warm welcome!

A few new teachers were on the same flight as I was. As we waited for the teachers to clear customs, the director took me aside to tell me that we were being housed in the same complex I'd lived in before the war. I was happy to be going back into a familiar area, but at the same time, I sensed a warning in the director's words.

The drive from the airport to the apartments in Fahaheel was uneventful. There wasn't much to see because we were on the ring road and it was dark.

When we arrived at the complex, what stood before me made my heart stop. I knew that the invading forces, as well as many others, had cannibalized the three apartment towers. I also knew that soldiers had taken several of my former colleagues from these apartments during the war and had held them as hostages. It was these memories that came to me at that moment, as well as the impact of the war.

What was before me were the three towers. The middle tower had been repaired and renovated, and the other two towers still held the war scars.

It was the same, but not the same.

The school director, tactfully settled the other teachers in before he took me to my apartment.

I entered an apartment that was very familiar to me because the layout was exactly the same as my previous apartment. It was incredibly eerie, like a moment of déjà vu, but not.

I stood in the living room and dining room area, letting the emotions flow through me.

The director stood behind me in silence. And then he gently asked, "Are you okay?" It was at this moment that I understood why he gave me the warning at the airport.

He and a couple of other Kuwaiti friends stayed with me for a while to ensure that I was OK. We shared our experiences of the past three years. When they left, I stood at the window looking out at the waters of the Gulf and at the skeletal building across the way, and I reminded myself that I wanted to return and there I was!

Nothing could've prepared me for this experience. Some things just have to be experienced in order to be understood.

The next day, Tareq, the accountant from the school, took all of us teachers to the market to do some shopping. As we drove around, evidence of the war was everywhere: in the tank tread marks on the roads, in the remains of the bombed buildings, in the air missile launchers still in place and ready for action, in the burnt-out vehicles and tanks, and in the ever-present rubble. All of this once again brought the reality of the situation into my awareness. Over the next three years, much of the destruction was repaired, but those visions of the destructive nature of war remain.

The one place that hadn't changed was the school. Al Bayan Bilingual School had escaped destruction. It felt good to be back in this familiar setting. However, it was pure joy when so many of my Arabic colleagues that I'd known before the war greeted me. Among them was my dear friend Abdul Ghani! It was like a homecoming.

When the students returned in September, many of them welcomed me back like a long-lost friend, especially those I'd tutored before the war. It didn't take long for them to invite me to their homes and to resume tutoring.

The school, staff, and students helped to create balance for me. Before long, I adjusted. It also helped that a friend lent me a vehicle for several months, and I was able to visit friends and to explore on my own. Eventually, I had my own car.

Although my physical world adjusted, my inner world hadn't. The day of Aug. 2, 1990, had changed me.

I was the party girl as a teenager and into my 20s and 30s. My social scene revolved around alcohol. That all changed after 1990. In Malta and Lesotho, I realized I no longer wanted to be that person. The social scene in both those places helped me to start making the changes I needed.

But my return to Kuwait landed me back in the party world. Although Kuwait was considered a dry country, it was anything but dry. Alcohol flowed freely behind closed doors.

Abstinence became an inner struggle for me. I didn't know how to socialize without drinking. I didn't know how to be myself. I was in uncharted territory. I wanted to change and didn't know how. I socialized with colleagues and friends but tended to refuse invitations to large parties. As a result, I often spent a lot of time alone.

Expats usually socialize with the people from their workplace and with their friends. If you aren't part of this group, you can become isolated. At times I felt isolated. I never spoke about this to anyone. Instead, I stewed in my negative thinking, wondering what was wrong with me.

I presented a self-confident and happy self to the world, but that wasn't what was happening within me. I was swirling in my cauldron of self-doubt and self-pity. I felt stuck and didn't know how to get out of my funk. This was a very dark time for me.

I knew there was more. I'd experienced the flow and ease of life when I was backpacking. I wanted to get that sense of flow again.

With hindsight and with what I know today, I'm sure that post-Gulf War Kuwait's energy added to my own confused personal energy. I was mourning the loss of my old self, much as Kuwait was mourning the loss its old self. My inner energy mirrored the energy of the recovering country.

But even though I thought I'd lost connection to my inner guidance system, it was still there looking after me.

A couple of things happened that began to pry me out of my funk. One was when the high school moved to a new site. The new campus was in an older Kuwaiti government school. This move completely changed the school's atmosphere. The energy at the new site was very different from the energy of the original site. Even though we were still one school, a divide was created between the original Bayan and the new Bayan. The new site didn't have the warmth, community spirit, and vibrancy of the original site, and it began to affect me. I was starting to lose the spark for what I was doing.

The other thing that happened was that someone gave me a book called

Feel the Fear and Do It Anyway by Susan Jeffers. One of the first exercises in the book was to write down 100 things that made you grateful. I followed her instructions and bought a beautiful notebook and a Waterford pen to create my list. This exercise completely shifted my thinking. I didn't stop at 100 things that made me grateful; in fact, I wrote almost 400 things! Every day for a couple of years, I wrote down five things that made me grateful. My mindset began to change and the clouds of darkness began to disappear.

Another book that came into my life at this time was The Celestine Prophecy by James Redfield. This particular book helped me to look at my life and see how I was divinely guided each step of the way. This insight opened up an inner light within me and catapulted me out of my despair. The connection with my internal source returned, and I knew what I had to do.

Shortly after that, I began to use guided meditations, which eventually led to meditating on my own. It wasn't long before I started to notice changes in both my inner world and my outer world. The inner turmoil began to recede, and a new inner peace became the norm.

With these changes, in 1996 I decided to return to Canada.

# Chapter Twenty-Eight
## I'm Not Quite Ready Yet

O ver the years, I returned to Canada for a month or more to visit family and friends about every second year, but always with the surety of an airline ticket to my next destination. In the summer of 1996, I went to Canada without my escape ticket to somewhere else. I'd obviously changed.

Up to this point in time, I held an unspoken fear of being stuck in Canada and not travelling. Travelling was my freedom! My unique sense of self! My identity, after all: I was a free-spirited wanderer!

Several years before this, I had an insight where I realized that the person who I was in Canada with my family was completely different from the person who I was out in the world. When I was around my family, I immediately became the insecure, people-pleasing little sister. Whereas when I was away from my familial and cultural conditioning, my true self was allowed to shine.

The decision to return to Canada was a huge step for me. My inner guidance system was pulling me to take that step, and I was willing to follow. As with most of my sudden shifts in direction, I had no idea where I'd live, what I'd do, or how long I'd stay. I just knew that I had to follow my inner guidance.

For the first couple of months, I stayed with one of my sisters in Edmonton. It was summertime, and I fully enjoyed visiting with friends and family. There were outings at the lake, barbecues with family and friends, and family time around the fire pit. I also spent time with my dad picking berries, tramping in the forest, going fishing, and playing cards.

In September, I moved in with Karen in Calgary. I started applying for jobs, and even though I was shortlisted for several, I didn't secure a job. As I scanned the newspaper for employment opportunities, I came across a notice for a Life Skills training course in Calgary in the upcoming months. Since no jobs were coming my way, I thought that the Life Skills course might open some doors and I applied.

Although I made an effort to resettle in Canada, the pull of the world-at-large was tugging at me. It wasn't so much that the fear of being stuck in Canada had returned, but more of an "I'm not quite ready yet" to live in Canada.

In November, I started the process of attending another job fair. This job fair was with a different agency and in the U.S. I was going to Seattle, Washington, in February of 1997.

Right around this same time, I had a profound experience while meditating. At that period of my life, I meditated every morning after I woke up and every night before I went to sleep.

On this particular night, I settled into the meditation feeling grounded and calm. Several minutes into the meditation, I saw a brilliant red light come to me, and then I heard my deceased mother's voice.

From the time I was nine years old, I had a love-hate relationship with my mother. It began on the day we received the news that my older brother died in a car accident. On that day I not only lost my brother, but I also lost my mother. From that day forth, my mother entered a state of deep grief that was ever-present, leading to her alcoholism.

I carried anger at my brother for taking my mother away from me and at my mother for being so wrapped up in her grief. The little girl within wanted her mother to return.

My mother did return.

I no longer recall the exact words that she spoke, but I do remember the gist of that conversation. She expressed a deep love for me and my siblings and said that she never meant to hurt anyone. She asked for forgiveness, and I willingly gave it! As powerful as these assurances were, her explanation of what she'd gone through was even more enlightening. She had felt trapped, and as much as she wanted to, she couldn't find a way out. When she finished talking, the red light turned into a brilliant white light, and she left.

I've no idea how long this conversation lasted. After she left, I sat, feeling loved and more at peace than I'd felt for many, many years. I just sat in the glow of love and forgiveness. My inner pain was gone. I was lighter.

After the experience with my mother and applying for the job fair, I decided to take advantage of the time to do some things just for myself. I took watercolour painting and sketching classes, which revealed creativity that I never knew existed. I got into bread making and created delicious vegetarian meals for Karen and myself. I also completed the Life Skills course.

In February, I flew to Seattle with two friends to attend the job fair.

I planned to have some fun exploring Seattle with my friends as well as securing a job. That's exactly what I did!

Once again, my Divine Guide made it clear as to where I'd be going next. When I opened up my recruitment package, there were three interview invitations with three different schools in Bangkok, Thailand. The directors of two of the schools were people that I'd worked with in Africa. These interviews were more social than professional. Although it was great to reconnect with those I already knew and to be guaranteed a job, I had to choose only one school.

I chose the one that had the greatest potential for career advancement.

In August, I was on my way to Ruamrudee International School (RIS) in Bangkok, Thailand.

I was excited to be returning to Bangkok after a 10-year absence. My return was now as a professional international educator rather than a backpacking traveller.

Wow, this girl came a long way!

What awaited me in Thailand?

# Chapter Twenty-Nine
# What Is Success?

Nothing stays the same, not even ourselves. That's the nature of life! The constant flow of energy brings new experiences to help us grow, evolve, and expand. Each moment, we're a new person in a new time and space.

As I boarded the airplane for Bangkok, I was a different person from the woman who arrived in Canada in 1996. The time I spent in Canada gave me a glimpse of what it'd be like to live there and planted seeds of possibility. However, it would take a few years of germination before the seeds would take root.

I arrived in Bangkok lighter, freer, and connected with my inner guidance system. My self-confidence had returned, and I looked forward to new adventures.

Once I settled into my new apartment, I began to re-explore the city that I once knew. I went back to the area I lived in 10 years ago. Just like myself, it too had changed. A new generation of travellers had brought different needs and expectations to Khao San Road.

Although I was saddened to see some of the changes, I fully understood that nothing remains the same and that change can be good.

Some things in Bangkok still remained the same. I treated myself to a Thai massage at Wat Pho. Then, I visited the Grand Palace, the temples of Wat Arun, Wat Phra Kaew, along with some other sites. It never ceased to amaze me that once inside these temples, the noise of a busy city faded away and was replaced by peace and quiet. Whenever the people, noise, or chaos that is Bangkok became too much, I could find refuge in the temples' stillness.

I explored the shopping area along Sukhumvit Road as well as the markets and the alleys of Chinatown. Bangkok is a shopper's paradise. Although I enjoyed exploring the markets, I'm not a shopper. I just enjoyed watching the people and feeling the sense of aliveness in a busy outdoor market.

I reacquainted myself with the water taxis on the Chao Phraya River, and I became familiar with the *klong* taxis (boats). *Klongs* are canals that branch out from the river and run throughout the city as roadways.

I lived in a northeast suburb, a different area of Bangkok than I was accustomed to. So, it was during these outings that I discovered the quickest and easiest ways to navigate the city.

Shortly after I arrived, I purchased a motorcycle. Not a big monster bike that you see on the roads in Canada, but a small one, about the size of a Vespa. On my motorcycle, I could easily weave in and out of traffic in my community and the surrounding area. It sure beat sitting in a car waiting for traffic to inch forward. If I took a taxi into the city centre, I always had a book on hand, a bottle of water, and plenty of patience. Arriving late to an appointment wasn't unusual.

I settled into Ruamrudee International School with ease. Despite its large size, it had an open, friendly community atmosphere, and it didn't take long to become part of the Ruamrudee family.

Most of the staff lived in one of two communities near the school and a bond quickly developed among us. A few times a week, we met at one of the many outdoor restaurants in the neighbourhood for dinner. Eating out was the norm rather than the exception, as dining out was inexpensive, healthy, and delicious. And a lot of fun!

The personal changes I'd experienced in Kuwait and Canada had transformed me into someone who could socialize and be my joyful self again.

I enjoyed going out with the group to nightclubs and following my friends in a rock 'n' roll band. I took up golfing and especially relished the golfing weekends at various resorts with colleagues. Plenty of weekend getaways were available to various parts of Thailand, and I experienced things like renting a houseboat on a lake, sliding down a waterfall, or visiting a remote temple.

The party girl persona was gone, and the woman who loved to go out and have fun had returned. Moments of self-doubt and insecurity still emerged, but they never lasted very long. I felt alive and vibrant again. I loved life!

My career as an international educator also took off. The high school principal hired me as the English department coordinator. After a few years of teaching history and social studies, it was refreshing to teach English once more. The upside of being a high school English teacher was witnessing the creativity arise in my students. The downside was marking a never-ending stream of essays.

During my first year at the school, the administration began the process f adding an IB component to the curriculum. Because of my previous xperience in the IB program, administration invited me to be part of the eam spearheading its integration into the school. This took me from the English department and into the leadership role of IB coordinator.

It was a challenging year getting all the facets of the program into place nd convincing all the doubters that it would be great for our students and he school. However, I'm always up for the challenge. I thrive on change nd learning new things!

As if this wasn't challenging enough, an administrative position opened up at the end of the second year. The high school principal resigned, nd the assistant principal stepped into that role. Staff could apply for he assistant principal position before the school looked elsewhere for andidates.

I applied and was hired. Thus began my two-year stint as an assistant igh school principal.

I soon discovered that the vast majority of the school's problems, lisputes, and discipline landed on the assistant principal's desk. I was the peacekeeper as well as the disciplinarian. In my role, I got a glimpse of a eeper layer of Thai society, one that a visitor to Thailand rarely sees. The ace we show the world often hides what we don't want the world to see. 'hat was no different in Thailand.

With a high school population of 700 students, 70 teachers, and a large upport staff, there was a constant stream of issues. The life skills coaching took while in Canada was used daily with the conflicts that arrived in my ffice.

This was an amazing opportunity for me to clearly understand my kills and talents. It also provided me with a glimpse of how our social onditioning doesn't always jive with a person's natural self.

I was conditioned to believe that one should have a career and climb 1at career's ladder. I was taught that this approach was the key to success, ut what is success? Is success the last rung on the ladder, or is success vhatever brings joy and aliveness to a person at any rung on the ladder?

These were questions that I started to ponder.

The role I assumed as an assistant principal was an uneasy one. On the ne hand, my ego was strutting around filled with pride and saying, "Look t me, look at how successful I am!" And on the other hand, my inner uidance system was whispering that perhaps this role wasn't meant for me.

From that came the conflict between my ego and my inner self. The ego said if I quit, I'd be a failure; my inner self urged me to let it go. In the end, the inner pull guided my way.

I did struggle a little as my insecurities surfaced. To quell those insecurities, I applied for other administrative positions and was invited to a few interviews at schools in Asia. In hindsight, it was a blessing that I wasn't hired for any of the positions.

Since I wasn't yet ready to leave the world of International Schools, I went to one more job fair. I secured a job in a country that I'd wanted to go to since I was a teen. A lifelong dream was fulfilled!

I was going back to Africa. Oh, Mama Africa, you're in my blood!

# Chapter Thirty
## Excitement, Sadness, and Connection

I returned from the job fair in the spring of 2001 filled with excitement, and I began preparing to move back to Africa. Not only was I returning to Africa, but I was also finally going to set foot in a country I'd wanted to visit since my early teens.

A few weeks before I was to leave Bangkok, I received an email from home that put a damper on my excitement. In this email, I learned that my beautiful young niece had been diagnosed with ALS and that she was in an ICU unit in a hospital.

I planned to spend the summer in Canada before continuing on my way to Africa, and my niece's illness made me eager to be there with my sister and her family. That summer, I spent as much time as I could with my niece. The form of ALS that she had was rapidly moving through her body; thus, I knew that our time together was very precious.

Sometimes in life, we're given the gift of time, and sometimes we're not. For the next three years, I returned to Canada often to spend time with my niece and support her family. I'm very grateful for this gift of time and the precious moments we had before she left us.

In mid-August, I boarded a plane with my two cats and began the journey to Ethiopia. I first heard about Ethiopia as a young girl in a tiny church in a small village in northeastern Alberta. This small church had three missionaries in Ethiopia, and every few years they'd come back to Canada with their stories. I recall being a sponge and taking in their every word. Through their stories, the seeds of Ethiopia were planted in me. Over the years whenever I went to a job fair and saw Ethiopia on the list, I requested an interview. I never received one until this time.

I arrived in Ethiopia as it was recovering from the *Derg*, a 17-year period of communist rule that ended in 1991. The physical and emotional scars on the land and its people could be seen everywhere. Everyone I spoke with had a heart-wrenching story to tell. Yet, the inner light of the people was in their smiles and radiated from their eyes. They were slowly letting go of their fear and rebuilding their lives.

Initially, on the various excursions around Addis Ababa, I doubted my ability to adjust to the poverty and scarcity that I witnessed. I even questioned my decision to be there. After a pampered few years, I was once again faced with a bout of culture shock.

How would I ever find my way around Addis Ababa without any street signs or maps? In those days in Ethiopia, there were no cell phones, telephone booths, or any other means of contacting someone if I was lost or needed help. Considering all that I'd been through up to this point in my life, I have to laugh at how insecure I felt those first few months in Ethiopia. But then, culture shock is real, and so is reverse culture shock when you return to your home country. I experienced both.

Needless to say, it didn't last long.

I purchased a Suzuki Vitara four-wheel drive, and I was soon able to navigate around the city and avoid the crater-like potholes, the goats and donkeys, and the people who darted out into traffic. I discovered the various markets, coffee roasters, and cafés. I had help finding these places with my companions, Diane and Anna. Both these ladies worked at the school and were from North America. Diane had lived in Addis Ababa for almost 18 years and Anna had lived there for several years. Both these ladies were married to Ethiopians, which quickly helped me adjust to Ethiopia's culture, food, and nuances of life.

After getting comfortable driving in the city, I began to venture out of the city. One of our favourite places to go for the weekend was Lake Langano. At only 200 km from Addis Ababa, its lakeside cabins were old and needing some repair, but were fine to stay in for a few nights. The lake was also parasite-free, unlike some other lakes in Africa, so we could swim and enjoy the beach. The waters were a milky colour and believed to have healing properties. We spent many wonderful weekends soaking up the sun and relaxing on the beach.

Sodere was another place I loved. It's a resort that contained a hot spring pool. The resort hadn't been well maintained during the *Derg*. As a result, it was a bit dilapidated; however, soaking in the pool was divine. The restaurant wasn't very good, so we brought our portable barbecue and created delicious meals in the garden. Often we were the only ones staying in the hotel and got to know the staff on a first-name basis.

Sodere is also the place where I met a *sangoma* (medicine man).

I met this *sangoma* through my friend Melaku. One day, I mentioned that I'd really like to meet a local medicine person and Melaku said he knew one. By this time in my life, I was connecting more deeply to my spiritual side. I was meditating longer and searching for something I couldn't quite put my finger on. I knew that something was stirring within me, but I didn't know what it was. I was also developing a keen interest in shamanism.

The next time we went to Sodere, Melaku, Tamaru, and I went to see the sangoma. We headed down a narrow road that eventually brought us to a boulder-strewn dry riverbed. I looked at it, stopped the vehicle, glanced at my friends and said, "How am I supposed to drive through this?" They both laughed. Then Melaku asked if I wanted him to drive. My answer was a resounding "Yes!"

I held on for dear life as Melaku navigated the boulders. As we bounced from boulder to boulder in my four-wheel drive, I imagined us getting hung up on a boulder or worse.

But we didn't! We arrived at the base of a hill in one piece. Snaking up the hillside was a stairway carved in the earth, and at the top of the stairway stood a giant of a man. Yup, there was the sangoma!

Melaku exchanged greetings with him, after which we were invited up to his house. Once we were seated in his circular meeting room and introductions were made, his wife arrived with *Bona Maflat*, the traditional Ethiopian coffee ceremony. While his wife prepared the coffee, the *sangoma* told us that he had a dream that he'd get a visit from a white woman. He proceeded to ask me a battery of questions, which my friends patiently translated. Some of the translations required a discussion amongst the three of us because some of the sangoma's concepts weren't easily translated. And some my answers also needed clarity, as neither of my translators were familiar with some of the spiritual concepts I was trying to share. At the end of our visit, the *sangoma* told me that I needed to return to perform a ceremony with him so he could give me a message that he'd received.

A few months later we returned. This time we were ushered into the ceremonial house. Once more, we sat in a circle while the *sangoma* drummed, chanted, and went into a trance. When he came out of the trance, he had a message for me. Part of the message relayed to me was that I'd chosen a difficult path but that I'd fulfill it.

Almost everything that was told to me during that visit so far has come true. Time will tell if everything else will come to pass.

I went back to see the *sangoma* one more time. This time, I drove over the boulders while my sister and my cousin held their breath and told me I was crazy. This was a social visit, as we brought two huge bags of clothes for his family. Once more, with Melaku as our translator, the *sangoma* asked my sister and cousin many questions. He also told us that things were changing in the area and that he might have to move to another location for safety. A deep sadness was in him at this time. Shortly after this visit, I was informed that the *sangoma* had indeed left the area. I've often wondered where he went and thought about the welfare of him and his family. Sadly, age-old tribal rivalries and outside meddling have caused so much pain and hardship for the people.

My role as the IB coordinator in the school opened up opportunities for me to connect with the people in rural communities. Part of the IB program required students to do community service work. One of the projects I initiated was building houses with Habitat for Humanity. During the three years I lived in Ethiopia, the students and I volunteered our time one Saturday a month to build houses in three different villages.

Building houses in Ethiopia consisted of manually making adobe bricks. We spent many long hours sifting sand and then mixing the sand, concrete, and water in an open pit, then pouring it into the brick-forming machine. It was hard, back-breaking work. We then laid these bricks out in the sun to dry. When they were dry, we'd form a human chain stretching from where the bricks were located to where the family was building the house. We passed the bricks one by one along this chain until they reached the house. To break up the monotony, we'd sing songs, crack jokes, and laugh together. We tried not to think about our aching muscles.

The work to build a house was labour-intensive and time-consuming, but when the house was completed, there was so much joy to be shared as the family moved in. The family always invited us to the moving-in party. It left me with such a wonderful feeling that this family now had a solid roof over their heads. Each month I looked forward to the time spent with the family whose house we were helping to build, and to the camaraderie of the entire group as we worked on these projects.

Over the years I spent in Africa, I saw many projects being created by various agencies and non-profit groups. Not all projects were successful, helpful, or completed. Some of the projects even cause more harm than good. Habitat for Humanity is one organization that does what it says it will do, and as a result, many people around the world have a home.

As I connected with the people on the grassroots level and delved into the history of the country, I sensed there was something rich and deep in this land. Ethiopia had a completely different feel than the rest of Africa. I was keen to do more exploring and visiting in the place that I'd been reading about. I was drawn into the heart of Ethiopia in a way that I wasn't drawn into other countries.

# Chapter Thirty-One
# A Night of Sobbing and a Wet Pillow

The wonders and mysteries of ancient civilizations, which left a trail of artifacts and structures, fired my imagination and curiosity. The more read about Ethiopia's history, the more I felt there was so much more to his ancient land than we'd ever know.

Ethiopia, located in the Horn of Africa and as the source of the Blue Nile River, connected with Egypt and the Far and Middle East via the caravan outes that crisscross northern Africa. For me, Ethiopia didn't feel like Africa! Even now, as I sit here in an attempt to write these feelings, words scape me, but a sense of wonderment and mystery courses through me.

It could be that, unlike much of Africa, no European country fully olonized Ethiopia. Italy occupied Ethiopia for a short time between 1935 o 1941 but never got a strong foothold. It has remained an independent ountry.

So, when Anna asked me if I wanted to join her on a bus trip to thiopia's most famous historical sites, my answer was a resounding yes.

As I mentioned in the previous chapter, there were no road signs in he entire country. This was a remnant from the *Derg*. Road signs were emoved to make it difficult for people from various regions from moving round. A system of roadways existed, some in good shape and others in errible shape. Unless you knew the roads and where they led, you could ave an interesting time wandering around the countryside.

As a result I was eager to this trip organized by an American lady narried to an Ethiopian. It was another adventure on a not-so-modern bus vith a group of adventurous people.

No restaurants or rest stops existed between locations; thus, each erson brought food for lunch for every day of the tour. As a result, coolers, ood boxes, and luggage jammed the back of the bus. Washrooms were in he great outdoors with few trees to hide behind. Bathroom breaks were ften challenging because we drew a crowd as soon as the bus stopped n a seemingly unpopulated stretch of road, and because there were few rees, bushes of rock to squat or stand behind. However, using the Amharic he local language) word for bathroom was enough for you to get a little rivacy.

Each night, we stayed in small local guest houses in cities and ate breakfast and dinner in local restaurants.

In all the years that I've travelled by bus, it's the ones with the least comfort and the most challenges that I remember most vividly. A nice plush bus with comfortable seats and air conditioning doesn't make for a memorable moment.

Our first stop was in a city called Debre Markos. This wasn't a historical stop, but rather a stopover as it was halfway to the next destination of Bahir Dar.

Most of my travels up to this point had been in the eastern or the southern part of the country. What I found most fascinating was the large fields of grain still harvested by hand and ploughed by oxen, as well as the herds of cows and goats. When people think of Ethiopia, the image that often emerges is a barren land with no food, and yet I saw fields full of food.

I was eager to get to Bahir Dar because it's famous for two things: Lake Tana and as the source of the Blue Nile River.

Lake Tana is Ethiopia's largest lake. When the lake was calm, travelling in the small, motorized boat was a relaxing, beautiful trip over to the islands. But, if the wind picked up, it could be a white-knuckled ride as the boats were tossed around by the large waves. I experienced one of those white-knuckled rides with a friend and wouldn't want to repeat it.

Apart from its scenic beauty, there was a flotilla of papyrus fishing boats called *tankwas* which the fishermen used.

On the islands of the lake there are many churches and monasteries. We were able to visit the monastery of Ura Kidane Mehret, as it was the only one open to both women and men. This monastery dates back to the 14th-century and contains beautiful murals that date back 100 to 250 years.

For me, the allure of the lake and the islands was their ties to the Ark of the Covenant, which was purported to have been hidden in several of the monasteries over the years. I must admit, I was disappointed that we couldn't go to more of the monastery islands.

Not far from Bahir Dar is the source of the Blue Nile River. Standing above the Blue Nile Falls, I envisioned a boat journey from this point all the way down the river to the Mediterranean Sea. It seems that throughout my life, I've always been pulled to the road less travelled. If a road was off the beaten path, headed in a different direction, or went where others hose not to go, then that is where I wanted to go.

From Bahir Dar, our group made our way to Gondar. What stood out or me was the visit to the Debre Birhan Selassie church, built in the 17th-century.

This small church surrounded by a plain stone wall made me stop in ny tracks with my mouth open in awe. The walls and ceiling space were completely covered with painted images. But, it was the painted ceiling hat grabbed my attention. Above me were the faces of 123 winged cherubs whose eyes followed me around the church. It was a bit unsettling but so beautiful. As I moved around the interior, I felt a great stillness and inner peace wash over me. Very few churches had this effect on me. I can feel very uneasy in some churches. It's that same unsettling energy I can detect walking into buildings like a hotel, a hostel, or a store. This church was special!

Later, as I walked around the courtyard with its old gnarled trees filled with singing birds, I realized that I didn't hear any street traffic. All I heard were the birds.

I walked over to the courtyard gate, opened the door, and stepped over he threshold. Immediately, the cacophony of the street traffic assaulted me, but the moment I stepped back through the gate into the courtyard, all heard were the birds, even with the gate open. I did this several times, for couldn't believe my ears. As we left, I took that inner peace with me. This was one of my most memorable moments in Ethiopia.

As we left Gondar, we began the ascent into the Simien Mountains. The students from the school did a yearly trek to the Simien Mountains National Park. As for me, it wasn't on the list, at least not yet.

The journey through the mountains was spectacular, but then I have a special connection to mountains.

As we descended, we entered Tigray, the northernmost state that borders Eritrea. Our destination was the town of Axum. My travelling companions kept informing me that there wasn't much to see or do. However, I knew some of the history and was eager to explore.

It is said to be the home Queen of Sheba. It was part of the desert trade route that reached into the middle east. Today, it's believed that the Ark of the Covenant is in the church of St. Mary of Zion. With all this mystery surrounding this city how one not be inquisitive?

Unfortunately, when I was there, I could only stand outside the gates of the church and peer in; how I would've loved to get inside that church and see what was there for myself! It was another mystery that tugged at my curiosity!

My connection with Axum was powerful. When the others went off to eat or drink, I sat in various places and absorbed the energy. At a cellular level, I had a deep connection to Axum. I was blessed to have visited it twice.

The last stop on this adventure was the mysterious Lalibela with its 11 churches dating from the 12th and 13th centuries, and all of them carved deep into the stone of a mountian. No one knows who carved it or perhaps they do!

They're truly an amazing sight to see! However, this site affected me like no other site on Earth.

We arrived in Lalibela in the evening, went out for dinner, then went to sleep. I drifted into a deep sleep and awoke during the night by the sound of my own sobbing and the feel of my wet pillow. I had no recollection of dreams or anything else. As I sat there wondering what was going on, my tears kept flowing. I was filled with a deep sadness that seemed to have no explanation. By the time daybreak arrived, I'd stopped crying. My roommate woke up, looked at me with concern, and asked me what was wrong. I couldn't explain what happened because I didn't know.

We got dressed, went out for breakfast, and then met the group for our tour of the churches. As I walked down the stairs to the first church, I felt like I was carrying a huge weight. By the time we toured the third church, I knew I had to get out of the rock and away from the churches.

I found some stairs and climbed out of the cave. I walked away from the churches and sat in an area where I could look into the valley and the mountains in the distance. With my focus away from the cave and the churches, the weight lifted, and I began to breathe easily again. To this day, I've no idea what happened. I'd never felt anything like that before or since. I also know I don't want to feel like ever again.

It was interesting that one place filled me with peace and another filled me with sadness. I've always been tuned into energy and how things felt, but these experiences in Ethiopia showed me that I was tapping into the frequency of places, things, and people in a more acute way.

Everything carries a vibrational frequency. This frequency is neither good nor bad. It's just that some frequencies are heavier than others. My journey in Ethiopia gave me an experience at both ends of the frequency.

Although I felt a connection to Ethiopia, the inner struggle that began in Thailand between my ego self and my inner guidance system still played a tug-of-war within me. I felt that it was time to step away from international schools, but fear still held me back.

I let those fear rest in the back of my mind as I organized a safari in Tanzania for my friend Betty and myself. Little did I know it would the trip would bring me my most memorable safari moment.

I'd arranged a camping safari in the Serengeti. The Serengeti is one of the most famous parks in Africa. It's Tanzania's oldest park and a UNESCO World Heritage Site. This park borders the Masai Mara National Reserve in Kenya, and the two parks are home to the spectacular yearly wildebeest migration.

After wandering around the Masai Mara and other game parks, it felt appropriate that my most thrilling wildlife encounter was on this, my last safari in Africa.

Over the years, listening to the lions in the early evening as they walked around the veldt in search of food became music to my ears. I could tell how many there were, where they were, and in what direction they moved.

I love cats of all kinds, and to hear the lionesses in the wild as they walked around calling to one another while looking for food gave me a sense of connection to nature and to the lions. No other animal sound stirred me as these cats did.

On the second night in camp as we dined by candlelight, I heard the call of four lionesses as they began to spread out. I sat upright, went silent, and listened to the lionesses. Our guide noticed the change in me and asked me, "How many?" I whispered, "Four," and then pointed out the direction of each one. He smiled and nodded. We carried on eating dinner, but I was ever alert to where the lionesses were located. After dinner, we sat around and chatted for a while before calling it a night.

I couldn't fall asleep right away. I lay in my sleeping bag, listening to the night sounds, and eventually fell asleep, lulled by the magnificent felines. During the night, I woke up and needed to go to the bathroom. I sleepily crawled out of the tent and slowly made my way to the outhouse. As I rounded the corner of the outhouse, there before me, about eight metres away, was a lioness sitting and looking at me. I stopped and looked at her entirely without fear. Somewhere inside, I knew she wouldn't hurt me. We made eye contact for a few seconds, and I felt she was smiling as if to say, "And where do you think you're going?" I acknowledged that the outhouse was hers. Very slowly, I backed up until I was out of sight at the back of the building. Only then did I turn around and walk back to the tent. My call of nature was all but forgotten, and in its place was a sense of wonderment and awe.

As I climbed back into my sleeping bag, I pondered this encounter. It was so natural; the lioness and I were both creatures of nature. As we looked each other in the eye, we both knew we were kindred spirits.

What a magnificent gift this meeting was in that place, at that moment!

Africa, all of her, will always have a special place in my heart and soul.

Years later, when I told my dad this story, he smiled and nodded his head. No words were needed.

Soon after I returned from this safari, a random email changed my life.

# Chapter Thirty-Two
## An Amazing Birthday Present

As I was evaluating my role as a teacher as well as my life as a wanderer. I had a feeling that I was at a crossroads of sorts. With the benefit of hindsight, I can now see that this inner stirring began when I left Kuwait and returned to Canada in 1996. Some changes in my life were fast, and others were slow and took time to percolate and mature. This was one of those slow ruminating processes.

I was happy at the school in Addis Ababa and with my life in Ethiopia; however, I couldn't ignore what was happening inside me. I was reading voraciously during this period, gobbling up books on spirituality and shamanism, along with ancient philosophies like Buddhism, Taoism, and others. I was also tapping into my innate healing abilities.

I had powerful dreams and insights where I woke up with messages, like the one that bolted me awake one night yelling that it was all about thoughts. I not only heard the words, I also felt the truth within the words.

I began to pay attention to my thinking, which revealed thought patterns holding me back and keeping me stuck. The most interesting part of this process was that as soon as I became aware of a negative thought pattern and what it was doing to me, it disappeared completely.

My daily meditations connected me with something greater than myself. I always had a connection to this Divine Source. It was this source that guided me throughout my life. Despite this connection, there was a separation between myself and the source.

Like most people, I knew that God, the Divine, Great Spirit, or whatever name you give it, was somewhere out there, separate from my physical self. I had an intellectual awareness of the oneness rather than a deep connection to it. I had only fleeting moments when I felt that I was one with my Divinity. I knew there was more. I wanted more! More of what? I wasn't really sure.

Shamanism was the focus of much of my reading and interest. The visits that I'd had with the sangoma, the Ethiopian shaman, fuelled this interest. I began searching the Internet for a teacher or a guide. Several well-known shamans offered training over extended periods of time. One shaman in particular caught my attention, as Peruvian shamans had trained him and he shared the ancient wisdom of the Andes. However, his programs and courses never seemed to coincide with our school holidays.

That all changed on my birthday in February of 2003. I arrived at school early, as I usually did, and opened my email. The school had a much better Internet connection than my house, which wasn't really saying much.

In my inbox was an email from someone I didn't know. I don't recall what the subject was, but something caught my attention and I opened the email.

It read something like this: "Hi Carolynne, My name is Michael Smith, and I'm a friend of Stuart Wilde's. You recently purchased a book and spoke with Stuart. I know this isn't legal, but Stuart gave me your contact information as he thought you might be interested in my upcoming shamanic retreat in Brazil."

At this point in the email, he had my complete, undivided attention. As I continued to read, I began to feel like the universe had given me an amazing birthday present. My whole being was alert and awake.

I quickly checked the dates of the retreat. They aligned perfectly with our Easter break in March.

My first class that day happened to be a preparation block, so I had time to call my travel agent to inquire about flights from Addis Ababa to Itabuna, Brazil. Within half an hour she called me back, informing me that I'd need two extra days for the return flight. I asked her to hold the flights and that I'd call her back by the end of the day.

During my lunch break I went home, something I rarely did, to call Michael for more information and to ensure it wasn't a scam. It wasn't! I had a wonderful conversation with Michael and knew that this was something that I really wanted to do.

I went back to school that afternoon, taught my classes, and went to talk to the school director at the end of the day. As fate would have it, my director had taught in Brazil, so he had a fairly good idea about what kind of retreat I wanted to go to attend. However, I did need his permission to take two unpaid days at the end of the holiday. The school frowned upon staff taking extra days at the beginning or the end of school holidays. I can recall brazenly informing him that I would take those extra days whether or not he approved. He gave me the permission I needed.

I called the travel agent and booked my flights, only to discover I had one more hurdle to overcome. I needed a visa for Brazil, and the closest

Brazilian embassy was in Kenya. I had less than one month to obtain this precious visa. The travel agent arranged for me to send my passport to Kenya via courier, then instructed a travel agent in Nairobi take the visa forms and my passport to the Embassy of Brazil, and then to send it all back to me.

The next several weeks were tense as I waited for my passport to return from Kenya. Would I ever see my passport again? Would I be given a visa? Would my passport with the visa come back in time for me to catch the flight?

Much to my relief, my passport with the required visa arrived three days before I was due to fly out. Talk about cutting it close! But then, I wasn't the one in control of this whole situation. Something greater than me was leading the way.

That same something also arranged for me to get my tickets bumped to first class on the flight from Johannesburg to São Paulo, Brazil.

I arrived at the resort in Brazil feeling tired but elated. The resort was a beautiful, Balinese-styled centre located on a stretch of near-deserted beach. It was literally a paradise.

Although I'd done some reading on the Internet and had an idea of what was getting myself into, I soon realized that I was stepping into a whole new territory.

This shamanic retreat involved ingesting a plant medicine called *ayahuasca*. I knew this when I made the arrangements to join the retreat, but it was when I spoke with the shaman that I realized the enormity of what I was about to do. I was curious, excited, and at the same time, terrified. I was a total novice when it came to mind-altering drugs. I may have grown up in the '60s surrounded by the drug culture, but the only drug I'd indulged in was alcohol.

*Ayahuasca*, a psychoactive brew, is grown in South America. The indigenous people of the Amazon basin use it in ceremonies and rituals. Although it's a psychoactive drink, it isn't addictive. However, I'd add that no one should enter these ceremonies without proper guidance and a clear purpose for journeying.

In one of my first ceremonies, I asked who I was as my intention. In the ceremony, I journeyed to my heart. I saw my heart open like a beautiful red rose, which proceeded to radiate this unbelievable love energy. I spent the whole ceremony engulfed in this pure, radiant love.

In another ceremony, I asked for guidance as to what I should do next. The first vision I saw was a room full of suitcases. I asked, "Where am I going?" I found myself sitting in an airplane and looking down on a huge city in a valley surrounded by mountains. I asked, "Where is this?" What appeared before me was a Vegas-style neon sign that read Cusco. I asked, "What am I supposed to do in Cusco?" The next moment, I found myself looking down on Machu Picchu. Again I asked, "What am I supposed to do there?" I saw myself with my arms around a huge rock. At the time, I'd no idea what it meant.

As a result of these ceremonial journeys, I decided to take a break from teaching and embark on a personal spirit quest. I'm sure it's no surprise that I chose to go to Peru for the beginning of my spirit quest.

Since I'd no idea how long I'd be or where I'd end up, I decided to downsize. I sold or gave away all of my possessions, except for two suitcases that found their way into my brother's basement in Canada and my trusted backpack that went on the journey with me.

Thus began my personal spirit quest!

# Part Four: Coming Full Circle

Walking away from a lucrative job and a successful career, and then giving away most of my earthly possessions wasn't as easy as it may sound. It brought up my deepest insecurities. A stream of "what if" thoughts swirled in my mind. I could sense my family and close friends shaking their heads. Despite all that, there was trust. I've always trusted my inner guidance system and was guided once more by insight. I'd no idea where this curve in the road would lead. Never in my wildest dreams would I've guessed the out-come.

# Chapter Thirty-Three
# Me Looking at Me

I was afraid! There, I said it.

Yes, as I prepared to leave Ethiopia, I was afraid. You're probably thinking, "What? After all the things you've done, you were afraid?" I was!

Although I was thinking this quest would be short-term, a year at the most, I sensed that this was a major turning point in my life. What came bubbling up during these moments of fear were my insecurities.

I think at times, I had my whole family in my head questioning what I was doing. "What? You're putting aside your career for a spirit quest? Are you really walking away from the place where you've always wanted to live and from a job that's providing you with a fantastic salary? When are you going to grow up? What about your retirement? Are you crazy?"

Perhaps I was crazy in most people's eyes, but despite the fear and the insecurities, this was something I had to do.

As I stepped around the fears, I organized everything, except for two items. I needed to book a hotel in Lima for one night, and I needed a place to stay in Cusco. Every time I opened the Lonely Planet guide for Peru to read about accommodations in Cusco, it opened on the page with a hostel called Casa de la Gringa. I read the review and saw that it was owned by a South African woman who was spiritually inclined and who also owned a travel agency. When I opened the book to check out other things in Cusco, invariably I came across the name Lesley Myburgh, Casa de la Gringa, or Another Planet Peru, her travel company. I finally admitted that I was being guided.

I whipped off an email to Lesley, explaining why I was coming to Peru and what I was looking for. She replied immediately, and before I knew it, she organized my overnight stay in Lima and booked a place for me in her hostel in Cusco. During my five years in Peru, Lesley, along with her family and staff, became an integral part of my life. We became soul sisters.

Even though I was jet-lagged when I arrived in Peru, I slept very little that first night in Lima. Perhaps I was too tired, too excited, or too scared. I'm not sure!

The next morning as we were making our descent into Cusco, I couldn't believe my eyes. As I stared out the plane window, I looked down at the very vision I had in Brazil the year before. The only thing missing was the neon sign that said Cusco. Any doubts I had about being guided by a divine plan completely disappeared.

I took some time getting acclimated to the altitude, culture, language, and temperature. The altitude wasn't too bad for me because Addis Ababa was 2,355 metres above sea level, and Cusco was 3,399 metres. It was harder for me to adjust to the language and the cold. Peru didn't have central heating, and the abode walls held the chill. I slept under a pile of heavy woollen blankets, and under my pyjamas I wore socks, a hat, and thermal underwear. With time I got used to it, but it initially tested my resolve.

For the first few weeks, I played tourist. I explored central Cusco on foot. It's a great walking city! I went horseback riding in the mountains above Cusco and felt like I was at the top of the world. I loved it! I had a private tour of the sites around Cusco: Sacsayhuamán, Tambomachay, the Temple of the Moon, and Q'enqo. I also took a trip to Tambopata National Reserve in the Amazon Basin. In a way, it felt like I was avoiding the place that was calling me the strongest: Machu Picchu!

On the day I went horseback riding above Cusco, I had the first of several profound experiences while living in Peru. I returned to the Casa de la Gringa, ate lunch, and then joined the other guests in the garden. The guests were at the end of a day-long San Perdo ceremony. San Perdo is a cactus native to the Andes Mountains. It's used by the local shamans as a traditional medicine in ceremonies.

I was sitting at a table chatting with a couple of guests. There was a lull in the conversation. I closed my eyes and entered a meditative state. I could hear people talking all around me while keeping my focus within me. Suddenly, a white bolt of light came down into the crown of my head and went straight through the centre of my torso. I couldn't move. I felt the intensity of the light getting stronger and stronger. I could hear a voice saying, "Hold it." I held the light until I couldn't hold it any longer, then I fainted. When I came to, Lesley was beside me, holding a damp cloth to my forehead. As I sat up, I felt nauseous and then vomited. To this day, I've no idea why it happened or what it was all about. I do know it was a very powerful experience.

After I returned from the jungle adventure in Tambopata National Reserve, I was ready to go to Machu Picchu. Shortly after I arrived in Peru, I told Lesley that I wanted to find a shaman who could teach me Andean shamanism. While staying with Lesley in Cusco, she introduced me to several different shamans. However, I didn't feel a connection with any of them.

So when I was ready to go to Machu Picchu, Lesley arranged for me to go on a regular tour of the site in the morning and to meet a local shaman in the afternoon. I was also going to be staying one night in the shaman's guest house. Although I knew I wanted to learn from a shaman, I was very nervous. I had some trust issues as I'd heard stories of women being taken advantage of by shamans, and I didn't speak Spanish. So before I would agree to anything, I wanted to check out the shaman.

That first train ride from Cusco to Machu Picchu was mesmerizing: the steep climb out the Cusco Valley, the fields of corn and quinoa, the colourful clothes of the local people, and the flora as we travelled beside the river and the mountains. As you may recall, I'm very visual. During my time in Peru, I made the journey many times and each subsequent train ride was just as mesmerizing as the first. I loved that journey!

I arrived in Aguas Calientes, boarded a bus, and headed up the mountain to the sanctuary. For me, there are two Machu Picchus: one is the sanctuary or ruins, and the other is the mountain. Hang in there; I'll explain about the mountain a little bit later.

My first view of the sanctuary brought tears to my eyes. I stood rooted to the spot and felt this immense emotion flow through me. I belonged there!

I was completely oblivious to the other 24 people in the group surrounding me. However, when I finally looked away from the sanctuary, I saw our guide looking at me with interest. Over the years, this particular guide and I became friends.

I've no recollection of the rest of the tour, except that I always lagged behind the group. The tour ended just before lunch, and I was to meet the shaman at one o'clock. I had just enough time to eat a sandwich and to go to the washroom.

The rest of the afternoon I spent with the shaman. This tour was very different from the previous tour. I was invited by the shaman to feel the energy at all the different places that we visited. I lay on rock altars in some places, sat on other stones, or just felt the energy with my heart and hands.

We crossed all the barriers during that first visit and went into places no tourist can get near today. No words can describe that first visit. The shaman's explanations were so different from the previous guide, and his reverence for the sanctuary was palatable.

Towards the late afternoon, we were sitting on one side of the sanctuary and looking towards the other side. We'd been meditating and upon opening my eyes and looking up, I saw a woman walking towards me. She was dressed in a white robe with gold lining. As she got closer, I realized that the woman was me. We were looking at each other. As soon as I had that realization, she vanished. I turned and looked at the shaman. Our eyes met, and he just nodded his head. We stayed in the sanctuary until it was time to catch the last bus down the mountain.

We arrived at the guest house to discover that the shaman's wife had prepared a meal for us. I was introduced to his family. Little did I know that before too long, I'd become one of the family.

After dinner, I walked along the river and attempted to get my logical mind around all the events that'd happened that day. Needless to say, it was a futile attempt. I returned to the guest house, where the sound of the river lulled me into a deep sleep.

In the morning, I ate breakfast with the family. I chatted with the shaman before he left for his office. As he was leaving, he turned to me and said, "I'll see you later." I thought it was a rather strange statement, as I was taking the afternoon train back to Cusco.

I spent the rest of the morning exploring the town of Aguas Calientes before returning to Cusco.

Within 10 days, I was back on the train, heading for a meeting with the shaman.

What he had to tell me wasn't what I expected.

# Chapter Thirty-Four
## You Have To Climb the Mountain

The pull to return to Machu Picchu and to speak with Juan was like a gigantic magnet. I surrendered to the pull, arranged a personal meeting with him, then booked a one-way train ticket to Machu Picchu. I'd no idea what to expect. I just opened myself up to whatever came from the meeting.

After I dropped my backpack off at the guest house, I walked to the plaza to meet him. As we sipped coca tea, I told him of the visions I had in Brazil, and he asked me a lot of questions. I also asked if he'd be my guide, my *maestro*. In between the questions, were long pauses as he consulted his inner guide. Eventually, he sat back, looked at me, and said we'd have to go and ask the mountain. He informed me that it wasn't Machu Picchu, the sanctuary, which called me; rather, it was the mountain, Apu Machu Picchu. He then turned in the direction of the sanctuary and pointed to a mountain towering above it. I looked up to where he was pointing and thought, "So, what does that mean?"

Before I had a chance to ask my question, he said we'd have to go to the top of the mountain and consult with the spirit of the mountain. In a ceremony, he'd seek guidance to see if he could be my guide. I looked back at the mountain, took a deep breath, and swallowed the lump in my throat.

I wasn't a mountain climber at that point in my life. I was more like a couch potato. What he was suggesting scared the heck out of me.

Yet when he asked if I could climb to the top of the mountain, my answer was yes. I prefaced it with, "As long as I can go slowly." He smiled back at me and said, "Of course." We then agreed on a date and a time.

Meanwhile, I stayed in Aguas Calientes and paid another visit to the sanctuary. That day, I let the sanctuary lead me and felt something stirring in my heart and soul.

On the appointed day at 6 a.m., we boarded the bus for the sanctuary. From Machu Picchu, we began the climb to the top of Apu Machu Picchu. As promised, we went slowly.

Our first stop was at the gateway to the mountain, where we asked the mountain for permission to climb and gave an offering. We also asked for a safe journey. We stopped at other places with breathtaking views of Machu

Picchu. Another important stop was at the heart of the mountain, where the mountain gave me a special gift of a large piece of Machu Picchu jade that I carry in my *mesa* (cloth altar) to this day.

Four-and-a-half hours later, we arrived at the summit. I won't lie to you; that climb up the mountain was a testament to how much I wanted my answer. It tested all of my inner strength as well as my physical strength. Over time it became easier, and I could do the climb in about two hours.

On the summit, the shaman immediately began to prepare for the ceremony. As he laid out his mesa, I watched as he called upon the spirits of the four directions, the heavens, mother earth (*Pachamama* in *Quechua*), Machu Picchu, and the Apus (the sacred Peru mountains). He then cleansed us with smoke. We were ready to begin. We drank a small amount of San Pedro and went into meditation. During the meditation, he chanted, drummed, and shook his ceremonial rattle.

A few hours later, he guided me over to another part of the mountaintop. Here, he shared the message he received.

He told me that I didn't need a teacher or a *maestro* because I already knew how to be a shaman. He said I just needed to listen to my own inner guidance and trust it. He indicated that the mountain and the sanctuary of Machu Picchu would help me to connect with my inner wisdom. This was not all what I expected to hear.

Then, he invited me to walk with him as an equal so that we could both learn from each other.

Thus began our friendship and five-year adventure together.

I joined his groups, and he joined mine when I began bringing groups to Peru. He took me to sites that most tourists never see. If I were curious about a place, he'd say, "Let's go." We spent nights on mountain tops, visited other shamans, explored the lower levels of Machu Picchu, and experienced other amazing adventures.

In addition to the bolt of light running through me and seeing myself, I had more amazing moments. Like the time we sat in a ceremony in Tiahuanaco, Bolivia, right under the gaze of the guards, who didn't see us until we packed our things and began to move on. Then, they blew their whistles and yelled at us. Becoming invisible and walking past guards or sitting in plain view with no one seeing us became commonplace.

I also had an out-of-body experience when I flew around Machu Picchu and zigzagged around the Guardian mountains: Apu Huayna in the north, Picchu Putucusi in the east, Machu Picchu in the south, and Viscachani in the west.

As I sat at the summit of Apu Machu Picchu, I'd often conjure several condors and watch them soar above me.

On the site of Aramu Muru, which is known as a door or a portal to other dimensions located on the shores of Lake Titicaca between the city of Puno and the Bolivian border, I had a unique experience. There are many legends and stories of individuals who've entered the portal and have yet to return. I was fascinated not only by the legends but also by the surrounding rock forest. At the end of a five-day expedition in Bolivia where I experienced a couple of *temazcal* ceremonies (similar to sweat lodge ceremonies) with a Bolivian shaman and my Peruvian friend, I stayed in Puno to visit Aramu Muru. I wanted to see and experience this site for myself.

I hired a taxi in Puno and headed to the portal. I wandered around the unique rock formations and then went to the door. I knelt in the doorway with my forehead on the wall and began to chant. After a few minutes of chanting, I felt myself tumbling through the portal. I hadn't gone far when an invisible hand grabbed me by the collar and pulled me out of the portal. As I exited the portal, I heard the words, "Not yet!"

In Markawasi, I had powerful visions of the immense pain and suffering in the world as I meditated with my back against the Monument to Humanity. This fantastic site is not far from Lima in the high Andes. Its a mysterious stone forest of incredible carvings. Did humans, nature or others make these carvings?

Wandering around this plateau was like walking in another world. I felt a sense of wonder as well as peace. The evening that I sat against the Monument of Humanity, witnessing the pain and suffering, I was also given the message that I'd be able to help ease that pain in the future.

Initially, all of these experiences made me feel special and important. My ego loved it and wanted more. I even thought, "Wow, this is what being a shaman is about." How wrong I was! It was more like a sound and light show, beautiful to watch and experience, but it wasn't the real thing. Wow moments don't last; a true connection to our inner source of wisdom does. Everyone is a shaman! We all have that connection to source, and we only have to open the door.

A shaman walks their truth quietly, trusts their inner guidance system, and gives from their heart without judgment or recognition. They don't need a stage to stand on. Many shamans don't even use the word shaman. They're just ordinary people walking in spirit.

I came to relish my time in the sanctuary or at the top of Apu Machu Picchu. There I was still, had a quiet mind, became aware of myself the observer, deepened the trust in my inner guidance, and paid attention to my body. Meditating in Machu Picchu, with hundreds of tourists wandering around, was a wonderful place to find stillness and peace amidst the crowds and the noise.

In between visits to Agua Calientes, I hung out in Cusco or the Sacred Valley. When I was around people and doing ordinary things, I was watching my thinking. I was being mindful of patterns and becoming aware of the ways that I kept sabotaging myself. It was fascinating to watch my mind as it became quieter and quieter. My ego was losing ground.

It was also interesting to watch how the power of my thoughts could make seemingly difficult things easy. For example, every time I had to go into a government office or an unfamiliar bank or place, I'd walk down the street, inwardly repeating, "I will easily and effortlessly get the papers I need. It never failed! I walked into the office, I discovered no lineup, received friendly and helpful service, I used correct Spanish, and I completed my task quickly. It amazed me when I heard others regale tales of horror about these offices.

Help arrived when I needed it, like the time I was walking in an alley on my way home. Not long after I entered the alley, I noticed two girls following me. My Spanish was good enough by this time to understand that they were planning to rob me. I kept walking, and I said to myself, "I don't need to be robbed again. I've already had that experience." Immediately after I thought those words, an older lady stepped out of her doorway and scolded the girls for following me. The girls scurried off, I thanked the lady, and I walked home with a smile.

As I became calmer and more at peace, I also trusted that everything was unfolding perfectly. This became very clear when I created Andean Triangle Spiritual Journeys, a group experience where I took people to what I considered to be the three sacred points of the Andes: Lake Titicaca, Machu Picchu, and the Amazon. Due to one article published in one magazine, for four years I had a steady flow of customers from all over the world. I never advertised, used marketing strategies, or sought out clients;

they found me.

Machu Picchu had my heart from the moment I saw her. Yet stirring inside me was the memory of what I experienced in Brazil. I felt the pull to go to the Amazon basin and experience the *curanderos* or shamans of the Amazon.

For my 50th birthday, I gifted myself a month-long retreat at a remote lodge on the Amazon River.

# Chapter Thirty-Five
# Alone in the Amazon

In February 2005, I was in a LAN Perú airplane with my nose pressed against the window, gazing in awe at the magnificent Amazon basin below me. I'd been on the Amazon River in Manaus, Brazil, but a bird's-eye view of it from the air defies words.

My destination was Iquitos. The only way to get to this Peruvian city was by air or by a long, hot riverboat ride from Pucallpa upriver. If I had a travelling companion, I might've considered the long boat ride; since I was travelling alone, I chose the faster, more comfortable, and safer mode of transportation. Perhaps as I was nearing 50 at this point in my life, I was making wiser decisions.

Perhaps!

I stepped out of the airplane in Iquitos into a blanket of hot, humid air, and I possessed the same starry-eyed naivety that brought me to Peru. Like so many others, I was searching for the magic formula that would bring me greater inner peace and calm. I was still trapped in that pseudo-spiritual belief that what I was looking for was somewhere outside of me. As a result, there I was about to begin the first of several sojourns in the Amazon jungle.

For my first adventure into the world of the Amazonian *curandero* (a traditional indigenous healer/shaman), I chose to stay at a lodge owned and run by an American. A key factor in choosing this particular lodge was my limited ability to speak Spanish. I needed to stay somewhere some people spoke English, since I wanted to make sure that I understood what people were saying and what was happening, and that people also understood what I was saying.

I wanted to learn about the plant medicines, the ceremony details, and the *curandero's* duties. I even envisioned myself as a *curandero* helping others to heal.

Another thing I wanted to experience was an Amazonian shamanic week of isolation at the time of my birthday. I've never been one to make a big deal about birthdays, but something inside me was telling me that I was at a major turning point in my life. Hence, the week of isolation during my one-month stay at the lodge.

During the solo retreat, I spent a week in a hut situated in a secluded area away from the main lodge. Meals were brought out to me and the *curandero* periodically visited me. I only emerged for evening ceremonies.

I absolutely loved that week. I spent much of my time lying in the hammock and listening to the sounds of the jungle. It didn't take long to distinguish monkey calls or bird songs. I enjoyed the sound of crickets chirping and frogs croaking. I felt the intense breeze as it whispered through the trees, and the rising humidity as it heralded a down-pour. I watched the play of light in the canopy as the sun traversed the sky. I journaled and I drew. Although the jungle surrounded me, I felt completely at ease. There was something truly magical about being surrounded by so much vibrant life.

When I returned to the accommodation near the lodge, I went for walks into the jungle with the *curandero*. He showed me how to identify different trees and plants used for different healing purposes. Copaiba oil is used to heal rashes and cuts, and can be ingested to treat certain ailments. I learned to identify the Sangro de Grado tree, to tap the sap, and to use the bark. He taught me to look at the shape of the leaves, as they often give a clue for their use. For example, a heart-shaped leaf is for the heart. I could identify the ironwood tree. If you were lost and clanged this tree with your machete, the tree would ring like a bell. If the locals heard it, they'd come looking for you.

On the shamanic side of things, I helped to prepare the ceremonial medicine. I picked the chacruna leaves, mashed the *ayahuasca* vines, learned the correct order to place the ingredients in the pot, and discovered the correct amount of time to cook the brew. I also learned how to use songs (*icaros*) to enhance the energy of the ceremony. My teacher was a Shipibo *curandero* who came from a long lineage of Amazonian shamans.

I engaged in long conversations with the American owner of the lodge about different herbal remedies and shamanic practices, and about his experience living in the jungle. He was a wealth of information.

It was while I was lazing in a hammock during the heat of the day that the idea of guiding people on a spiritual journey in Peru first began to take form. From these thought-forms was born Andean Triangle Spiritual Journeys, where I'd take groups to three major points: Lake Titicaca, Machu Picchu, and the Amazon.

The Incas regarded Lake Titicaca as the birthplace of its people. They also believed the world began there. It was at Lake Titicaca that my groups began to connect with the energy of water, mountains, and themselves.

Machu Picchu is where the Andes meets the Amazon Basin. It's shrouded in mystery and holds amazing energy, which affects all who visit. Here, a shaman guided the groups through the esoteric elements of the site, while encouraging the group members to establish a deeper connection with themselves via a San Perdro ceremony. It was two days of deep inner connection.

At the Amazon Basin, we felt the vibrancy of life and connected to our inner self in sacred ceremonies. In these ceremonies I assisted a *curandero* in the *ayahuasca* ceremonies.

Within this triangle was powerful energy for transformation and growth. Each person in the group left with a deeper connection to their inner selves, for that is where all healing takes place. It's holistic healing on the physical, mental, emotional, and spiritual levels. When we heal or unblock the energy in one area, it affects all other areas.

I was also learning as I guided these groups. I came to a deep understanding that all healing comes from within. I cannot heal anyone except myself. All I can do is hold a space of pure love for each individual so that their personal healing power can reignite. Each one of us is a healer; a healer of ourselves.

Over the next four years while I lived in Peru, I visited Iquitos frequently. I soon had a group of friends and acquaintances. They often invited me to their homes and I often met with them on the *Malecón* (walkway) for a meal, a few afternoon drinks, and a visit.

On one occasion, some friends invited me to their house on Itaya River, a tributary of the Amazon River. To say it was a house is stretching it. It was a raft with walls. The family's bedding and clothing were suspended from the ceiling in hammocks. In one corner was a space for cooking, and in the middle was a wooden bench and table, where I sat with the children. I chatted with their mother, who stood holding a machete beside a square hole in the floor. Each time a rat tried to climb into the room, she would whack it with the machete. She didn't kill them, but rather knocked them back into the water. Once again, I was humbled by the hospitality that I've always received from some of the poorest people on this Earth.

I felt comfortable wandering through Iquitos' Belen Market, where shoppers can buy anything, legal or illegal. I got to know the *curanderos* in the market and learned more about the healing plants from the Amazon. The healer in me was like a sponge absorbing the information.

Not surprisingly, I got to know other *curanderos* and joined them in ceremonies. My reasoning for checking out other shamans was to see the differences in the medicine and in the ceremonies. I was also honing my skills as a *curandera*.

It was from these ceremonies that I learned not all ceremonial medicines were the same. Some *curanderos* added other plants to the mix, which affected people in different ways. Some of these plants could be quite harmful. I also learned that honesty and integrity were lacking with some *curanderos*. The easy income and naive travellers made it easy for them to be less than honest.

From these experiences, I realized that everything I needed to grow spiritually was inside of me. I trusted my inner source more and more. I had a steady flow of insights that guided me. I listened to the subtle changes in my body. Those feelings that indicated "yes, all is good" or "no, stay away".

In February 2007, during another extended stay in Iquitos, I had a strong message that pulled me to return to Machu Picchu and to do a ceremony on Apu Machu Picchu for my birthday. I left the centre where I was stay at the time, went into town, and phoned the shaman in Cusco. I told him about the message I received, and he said to get back to Cusco where he'd give me further instructions. I heeded his advice and booked a flight back to Cusco.

What awaited me in Cusco was an interesting set of instructions and a very memorable ceremony.

# Chapter Thirty-Six
## I Sang and the Clouds Parted

It is amazing how one decision can set into motion a set of circumstances that can completely change the trajectory of one's life. I've seen this repeatedly in my life, where a thought or an idea bubbles to the surface of my consciousness, and before I know it, events and circumstances appear that lead me in a direction that I'd never have imagined. That's precisely what transpired when I returned to Cusco in February 2007. I knew that the ceremony on Apu Machu Picchu was significant and that it was a turning point, but not in my wildest dreams did I imagine where I'd end up.

As promised, my shaman friend presented me with instructions for collecting the items for the ceremony on my birthday. Some of the instructions were pretty straightforward, but some of them weren't. The most interesting instruction was to purchase a bottle of the first tapping of *chicha* (a *Quechua* word), a local corn fermented drink that is common throughout the Andes. The first tapping meant that I had to be at the *chichería* (a bar or brewery) very early in the morning to get the very first draft of chicha. I also had to purchase it on the morning that I departed for Machu Picchu.

Because of the drink's fermentation, I had to carefully carry this bottle of *chicha* in order to not pop the cork. Two *gringas* (another woman and I) travelling by local, long-distance taxi with a bottle of *chicha* under her arm elicited some interesting reactions. The taxi driver that drove us from Cusco to Ollantaytambo kept suggesting that we stop the taxi, get some glasses, and drink the chicha. He had no interest in the ceremony. He just wanted to help us drink the brew.

Cusco's main market is where I purchased the remaining items for the ceremony. In the *bruja* (pronounced BROO-ha and meaning witch) section of the market, I purchased a specific package of items for this ceremony. In this area of the market, I also bought three large San Pedro cacti. In a different section of the market, I bought some carnations and roses, a small bottle of wine, some incense, a bag of coca leaves, and a small bundle of wood. Fortunately, I travelled with a couple of friends, and we distributed the items equally in our backpacks.

Then, as I boarded the train for Aguas Calientes in Ollantaytambo with a bottle of chicha, a bundle of wood and three San Pedro cacti poking out from the top of my backpack, the porter, whom I luckily knew, shook his head. This wasn't the first time that I boarded the famous Peru Rail tourist train with interesting luggage.

When we arrived at the guest house in Aguas Calientes, I began to prepare for the ceremony. This involved a long, detailed preparation of the cacti that took most of the day and that went well into the night.

The next morning, I was wide awake at 5 a.m., even though I'd slept for only a couple of hours. Our small group, consisting of the shaman, three friends, and myself boarded the bus, which took us to the Machu Picchu Sanctuary. It's there that we began our climb to the top of Apu Machu Picchu.

It was a beautiful morning! The weather was absolutely perfect for this three-hour climb. The views of Machu Picchu were breathtaking as always, with wisps of early morning mist floating over the complex. Along the way, we stopped at various places to make offerings and ask permission from the mountain to do the ceremony.

We selected a place for the ceremony at the summit, laid out our mesas (ceremonial cloths), and prepared ourselves for the ceremony. As we were setting up, the mist started to roll in, and eventually, we were enveloped in cloud cover. Throughout the day, a soft drizzle of rain came and went.

Regardless of the weather, once the ceremony started, we kept going until it was done. At the end of the day, we were all soaking wet.

Since 2004, I'd been assisting my shaman friend in ceremonies, but this time he was assisting me.

I can recall being nervous, and at times I'd pause and try to remember what he had done during other ceremonies. At one point, he placed his hand over mine, looked at me, and said, "This is your ceremony, and you must do what you feel in your heart. You know what to do."

I did!

When I was in the Amazon rainforest where I had the vision for this ceremony, I was inspired to write a song honouring Machu Picchu and the surrounding mountains. As I stood on the precipice of Apu Machu Picchu, all I saw were billowing clouds obscuring the mountains and the sanctuary. With a sense of deep calm and gratitude, I began to sing. When I mentioned each mountain's name, the clouds opened up to reveal that particular mountain. It was as if the mountains heard me. When I came o the part of the song where I sang to the sanctuary of Machu Picchu, the clouds not only parted, but a ray of sunlight also shone through on the *Inti Watana*, an extraordinary part of the sanctuary. I kept singing as tears rolled down my cheeks. Tears of gratitude, love, and joy!

When it was time for me to create the *despacho*, an Andean-style mandala using various symbolic objects, it was raining, and we were soaked. Many of the objects used in creating the *despacho* were small, made from paper, and difficult to handle with wet fingers. Despite the rain and my ice-cold fingers, I created a beautiful *despacho* that came from the inner wisdom in my heart. This beautiful, magical place filled me with love, joy, and a sense of deep inner peace. I felt a deep connection to my inner source and to this amazing place.

When the clouds parted to my song that day, it felt like I created an opening to my true self. It was the beginning of letting go of my other self that had been created by past conditioning.

As I walked down the mountain with my friends, full of laughter and joy, I felt like a totally new person: centred, grounded, and whole.

Gradually, things started to change for me. In between guiding the spiritual journey groups, I was returning to Canada more often. A bit of a seesaw movement appeared to be happening. When I was in Peru, I was drawn to Canada, and when I was in Canada, I was eager to return to Peru. An inner tug-of-war was going on within me. I think I knew which force would win at a deeper level, but I wasn't ready to admit it. Slowly the barriers began to crumble, and I knew it was time for me to return home. It came to a peak one day while sitting in Machu Picchu with my friend when he said to me, "You can no longer have a foot in both countries. You have to make a decision." I replied, "I know." We both knew which world I'd chosen.

This seesawing between Canada and Peru lasted about a year and a half. When I returned to Peru in mid-May 2009 with a group to guide, I knew that this would be the last group I'd take to Peru. After 26 years of wandering the globe, I was ready to return to Canada. This traveller, who in the past was so adamant that she didn't want to live in Canada, was giving way to a version of herself who was much wiser, calmer, and centred.

As a farewell gift, Machu Picchu had one more surprise for me.

The day before my group and I were to leave Lake Titicaca, I had a frantic call from my travel agent in Cusco, who told me there'd be a major public transportation strike in Peru starting in two days. During the peak tourist season, strikes were a common occurrence because the strikers knew that the government would have to give in quickly in order to not disrupt tourism. My travel agent wanted to know if it was OK to change our itinerary to leave for Machu Picchu a day early. My answer was yes; otherwise, the group would miss out on going there. As a result, we had a speedy turnaround in Cusco and went straight to Aguas Calientes.

On the bus ride up to the sanctuary, the shaman was unusually quiet and had a twinkle in his eyes, which I'd come to know meant he was up to something. When we entered the sanctuary at a different entrance than usual, I knew something was up.

As I followed him through the twisting turns in the entrance, I was filled with anticipation. Whatever was awaiting us had to be quite spectacular for him to be secretive.

The moment I stepped across the threshold into the sanctuary was beyond belief. I stood transfixed, gazing out at a virtually empty Machu Picchu. Only a few people were walking around. It was quiet! There was only absolute beauty and stillness.

I couldn't move. I couldn't believe my eyes. It was like seeing Machu Picchu for the first time. Clean, clear, pristine Machu Picchu!

Standing beside me, my friend whispered, "This is for you! This is a gift for you."

And then tears began to flow in gratitude to this amazing place that had provided me with the space and time to shed so many layers of anger, fear, insecurity, and self-doubt. What I uncovered was who I really was behind the veneer. So much gratitude! So much love!

My shaman friend took the group on their tour, and I wandered through Machu Picchu on my own. It was like exploring this site for the very first time, unencumbered by thousands of other people. It was a most precious gift to be able to spend two full days in the empty sanctuary of Machu Picchu. This gift that touched my heart still brings me to tears.

I had a feeling that day that both my friend and the sanctuary knew that I'd be leaving and that I probably wouldn't be coming back.

A couple of weeks later, I was on a plane heading back to Canada. It was my place of birth, but in many ways, it wasn't my home. I had no expectations of what I'd do or how long I'd stay. All I knew was that it was time to return.

The fact that I'm still here 14 years later is something that would've never have crossed my mind in 2007. I truly believe that there's a much greater force than my personal mind guiding me through this experience of life. The more I get out of the way and let my inner guidance system direct guide me, the more amazing my life becomes.

I'm grateful that I listened to this guide that spoke to me as a teenager and led me on an amazing adventure around the world. I know I'm not done yet! There is more to come, and as always, I've no idea what it will be, and that's the beauty of life.

# Chapter Thirty-Seven
## This Time It Wasn't About Me

When I arrived back in Canada in June 2009, I came with the attitude that I was moving to a new country. In many ways, that's what I was doing. The Canada I left in 1983 differed from the Canada I returned to in 2009. I wasn't even sure how long I'd stay. My family wasn't sure how long I'd stay. They were placing bets on when I'd leave again.

But, life had very different plans for me. Of course, it did! By now I should've known!

Divine intervention had guided me back to my homeland at this particular time, and I was soon to find out why.

Five months after I landed back in Canada, my second oldest sister was diagnosed with Stage 4 lung cancer, and my world turned upside down.

When my sister first told me about her diagnosis, I went through a period of shock and disbelief before anger and deep sadness took over. I'd experienced those early stages of grief in the past, but it was very personal this time.

At the time, I asked the same question many others have asked: "Why?"

Cancer is a word none of us wants to hear. But, we do.

I was happy to be back in Canada and living with my cousin in the Kootenays. I was working at a couple of part-time jobs, I was making new friends, and I was starting to feel settled.

All was well, and life flowed smoothly until I received a phone call from my sister. With tears and sobs, she told me about her cancer diagnosis. I was stunned, even though I knew she hadn't felt well for quite a while. After receiving the news, I changed my plans and travelled to Alberta.

My sister, Aileen, was the centre of our family. Her home was where everyone gravitated, and as a kid growing up, I spent part of every summer with her family. We'd always been very close, and I often regarded her as a second mother because of our 18 year age difference.

I planned to stay in Alberta for a month or two to give her and her family moral support.

Well, one month became two, two months became four, and then the request came. "Would you please stay with me?" How could I refuse?

Several considerations flashed through my mind: I was single and had no obligations, my nieces and nephew had young families and jobs and my brother-in-law needed support. These thoughts made my decision easy.

Yes, I'd stay.

So began a two-year journey for my sister, my brother-in-law, their family, and myself. Over the next two years, my brother-in-law and I became the primary caregivers; me during the day and him at night, with added support from their children.

Personally, it was a time of great compassion and self-awareness. For the first time in many years, I focused entirely on someone else instead of myself.

During the journey with my sister through the highs and lows, the good and bad, and the happy and sad, I had to reach deep into myself. Being her caregiver was the most challenging thing I've ever done. I often had to remind myself that we aren't given more than we can handle.

In the end, there was a silver lining hidden in this challenging journey. After my sister transitioned back to spirit, I saw the many gifts of wisdom she'd given me.

It wasn't about me. Several times at the beginning of our journey together, I'd get upset, angry, or sad. My sister would look at me and ask, "Why are you upset? Are you upset for yourself or me? If you are upset for me, don't be. If you are upset for yourself, look inside to see why."

A lot of wisdom was in these questions. I discovered that my emotions were about me and for me. For example, when I was sad, it was for me. I didn't want to let my sister go. When I was angry, it was because I felt trapped. I'd always been a free spirit who lived spontaneously, but now I couldn't just up and leave.

Live life fully. None of us knows when or if illness or tragedy will arrive. Nor do we know when our time in this reality will end. Because of that knowledge, we shouldn't wait to live. Why defer a dream or wait to do something special? Why wait to feel alive and vibrant? So many people wait for the right time or until there's enough money. I've lived life fully. I took risks, went where others feared to go, and got out of my comfort zone. I've led a life with no regrets.

Don't be afraid to love and to express your love. I feel so blessed that I had two years to show and express my love for my sister. So many others aren't given that chance. The love I express now for my family and dear ones is much deeper than before. I say, "I love you" to each one often.

We enter the world with nothing, and we leave with nothing. At the end of our earthly journey, we go as we arrived. We don't take our body, house, clothes, cars, money, or gadgets. We take nothing. Why do we spend so much time and energy gathering and protecting things? I live simply, with only those things I need and use.

We aren't our physical bodies. We're spirits. Yes, it's true; we're spirits having a physical experience. My sister lives on in my memories. Since she departed, I've had many moments where I think, "She would've liked this." She would've liked that I'm sharing this with you.

I feel honoured that my sister asked me to join her for her last journey. Through it all, there were two journeys: hers and mine. Both were profound!

Every trial that comes our way is an opportunity to grow and thrive. It's all in the way you look at it. You can see it as a burden to endure or an experience to discover new treasures. It's all in our perception.

Life is a journey comprising of experiences that are designed to help us grow. Live life fully and passionately, enjoying what you find along the way. For you never know when that last breath will come.

# Chapter Thirty-Eight
# Letting Go of My Travelling Companion

2014 was a pivotal year for me. Several life-changing events occurred during my first five years back in Canada, and I became more settled. As a result, I began to let go of the things that were part of my wandering life.

Some ties were easy to let go of, while others were attached deeply to my image and releasing them was very symbolic.

The most symbolic item was my backpack.

Giving away a backpack wouldn't be significant for most people, but it was for me.

My backpack was wrapped up in my identity. It represented who I thought I was: a wanderer, a traveller, and a free spirit.

I felt that I was free as long as I had my backpack. I could pick up and go whenever I wanted. And I did!

But my life was moving in another direction. It was time for a new phase and a new focus. Besides, my back was crying, "No more!"

I decided to donate it to one of the many donation places in the city. As I placed the backpack in the donation box, I sprinkled a little traveller's dust on it so the next owner would have safe and happy travels. I also felt a tear trickle down my cheek as I let go of my companion.

My backpack was my companion when I discovered my identity outside my family, social, and cultural group. We don't realize how much our environment influences us. Early in my travels, I realized I was two different people. As I headed towards Canada, I would get a knot of anxiety in my solar plexus, wondering what was awaiting me. Approval or disapproval! I immediately became the insecure little sister about to face her older siblings. I hated that self!

The opposite happened when I boarded the plane to the next destination. Within moments I changed into the self-confident, curious, happy me. I knew which one I preferred, which could be one reason I was reluctant to move back to Canada.

It took years to let go of this perception and be myself. Now, I know who I am, and I'm very comfortable with that person. I don't rely on others for my identity.

With my backpack, I got used to being happy with less. You can only put so many items into a backpack. At one point, I lived for several years out of my backpack. During that time, my motto was, "If it doesn't fit, it doesn't go."

Little did I realize that this practice taught me the difference between needs and wants. Getting caught up in wants is so easy, which tends to clutter our lives.

Life is much simpler when we let go of our wants and focus on our needs. It's incredible how clearer and freer life is when we're not constantly worried about our possessions.

Home was where ever I was! With no permanent address, I used to joke that home was where my backpack was. All my worldly possessions fit into the pack for many years, so yes, it was my home.

I've become comfortable knowing home can be anywhere. Home, for me, is not a place, a building, or a location; home is where I am.

With my backpacking perched on my back, I experienced the ever-changing circumstances of life and the realization that I could adapt. I knew I'd be fine as long as I had my backpack and a few possessions. I was fine!

Things can and will be replaced.

This faithful companion and I had many adventures and experiences. We saw the sun rise over Kilimanjaro and came face-to-face with a lioness. We stayed in a houseboat on Dal Lake in Srinagar and drank chai in a riverside shack with a lovely family. We trekked to Machu Picchu and found a sanctuary where we could heal. We took a boat trip down the Amazon River and swam with the pink dolphins. We wandered around the Greece Isles, negotiated with thieves, traipsed through deserts, trekked in mountain ranges, swam in oceans, visited ancient sites and much more.

Lunging my backpack, I saw poverty, wealth, civil war, riots, and injustices.

On the other hand, many people showed me generosity, friendship, kindness, and goodness.

These experiences changed me indescribably and have given me a zest for life, a compassion for everyone, and a different way of viewing the world.

Experiences are the only thing we'll take when we leave this reality.

I learned the freedom that comes from trusting in a Divine Intelligence. As a child, I attended church until I realized I could talk to Divine Intelligence anywhere. That day at church, I knew I was never alone and could trust in this force. I learned to let go of control and get into the flow of life!

I surrendered the reins of my life to higher intelligence and began to enjoy the freedom of going along for the ride. This doesn't mean I don't plan; it does mean that I don't have expectations of how things should turn out. It does mean that I take full responsibility for my life and actions.

My backpack was my companion on this journey. It's been a journey with many ups and downs, tears and smiles, but most of all, it's uncovered the beauty in and around me.

The most significant part of letting go of anything is allowing something else to enter.

Yes, giving away my backpack was the start of a new phase of my life in Canada. Shortly after I put my backpack on the donation pile, my inner voice spoke to me again.

This time, the voice whispered, "Qigong, qigong, qigong."

Having lived several years in Asia, I knew what qigong (pronounced chee-gong) was, but where would I find it in Edmonton?

I began my search, as most people do, on the Internet. I came up with several tai chi classes, but no qigong. I let it rest, but the whisper persisted.

Then one day, I mentioned to a friend that I was looking for a qigong class. She immediately replied, "You need to find Dr. Aung." She'd taken some classes from him in the '80s and wasn't sure if he still taught the practice.

OK, I had a name, and the universe was doing its magic again because a few days later, I had a phone number for Dr. Aung after a casual conversation with someone else. I called him, and wouldn't you know, he was teaching a level one class starting on the weekend.

I attended the two-day training and, for several months, practiced with one of his qigong groups. I enjoyed the practice, but I sensed something was missing. Over the years, I learned to trust these feelings of unease.

I didn't have a long wait before another door opened. It came as an invitation to attend an introduction to something called Spring Forest Qigong. I was curious, and off I went.

While listening to the presenter and then actively practicing some movements, I knew this was what called me. On the spot, I signed up for more training.

What was it that spoke to me? First, it was the vision of grandmaster Chunyi Lin, the founder of Spring Forest Qigong, to have "a healer in every home and a world without pain and suffering." My vision was similar. I've seen so much pain and suffering in the world and feel it's so needless. I felt the words of his vision. Second, this type of qigong was created for everyone regardless of age, gender, or physical mobility. Third, it was simple and easy. My experiences have shown me things don't have to be complicated. If one keeps things simple, life flows more effortlessly, and this form of qigong fit the bill.

Right away, I started doing one of the movements every morning for 10 minutes. At that point in my life I wasn't a morning person, so 10 minutes was a stretch. Those 10 minutes became 15 , then 20, and I started to notice that I had more energy and was calmer. Some of my physical triggers disappeared, and my lower back pain from an accident and years of carrying a backpack eased. I couldn't wait to take the first training.

As my knowledge of qigong, healing, and Taoism grew with extensive training, I witnessed a significant transformation in my life and in others.

I became calmer, more peaceful, and trusted even deeper in my inner guidance. With a few gentle breaths, I can now enter that deep place where love, joy, and wisdom reside. Not much rattles me. That doesn't mean that life is all bliss and peace. I'm still human with the full range of human feelings. I can be vocal over injustices.

It means that I'm OK with whatever arises in or around me. I can acknowledge it, feel it, and let it pass. Once it passes, I know what action to take next or if I should let it go.

This was evident the day another driver broadsided my car, and then fled after he ran me off the road. Yes, I used my most colourful language and was angry as I watched him drive away. I sat stunned in my car as a string of inconveniences and problems streamed through my mind. Then, with a few slow deep breaths, I felt my body relax and my mind kicked into practical action. There was nothing I could do about the driver that disappeared around the corner, but I had to assess the damage.

As I walked around the car inspecting the damage, the driver behind me hopped out of her car and asked if I was OK. I said, "Yes." With amazement, she replied, "Are you sure? Because you don't look angry or upset." I smiled and said, "Oh, I was angry and I'm not happy, but the accident has happened and now I have to decide what I need to do."

All my plans for the rest of the day faded as I dealt with the police and insurance.

Qigong gives me the tools to keep myself centred and calm in unpleasant situations and keeps me healthy and strong as I age. The best part is that I help others stay healthy: physically, mentally, emotionally, and spiritually. Several times a week, I support a wide range of people to ease their pain and suffering by doing qigong. I'm also a trainer, teaching others to go out into the world and share the practice.

I love what I do, and I love life.

My life journey to this point has had a force of its own, and I don't doubt that more adventures await me. I love the idea of the unknown and vast possibilities, and I'm curious to see where I'm guided next.

# Biography

Carolynne Melnyk B.Ed, MA is a world traveller who currently lives in Alberta, Canada. She teaches English and settlement skills to newcomers in Canada. This is her way of thanking everyone who gave her so much as she meandered around the globe. She is also a certified Qigong trainer and, shares this ancient healing modality with several groups in her community.

Discover more about her Guided Insight mentoring and Qigong at her website www.livinglifeinjoy.com.

Made in the USA
Monee, IL
03 July 2023

38454377R00095